Houston, We Have A Problem...

A Humorous Account Of Some Of History's Most Embarrassing Moments

I0449018

Michael Polley

ISBN: 978-1-326-54040-1

PublishNation, London
www.publishnation.co.uk

Introduction

"I have not failed, I've just found 10,000 ways that won't work"
Thomas A. Edison

History is littered with the success stories and achievements of planet Earth's self-proclaimed intellectual masters, and to-date its most evolutionary successful biped. For many the peak of mankind's achievements was arguably squeezing some brave individuals into a tin-can, flying it to the moon, have them walk around a bit on its surface and then safely bringing them home again.

But, like the first humans to scramble up the side of Mt. Everest, doggy-paddle across the English Channel, or survive going over Niagara falls in a wooden barrel, putting a man on the moon to just stroll around for a couple of hours or so taking in the view was actually of little real benefit to science or mankind as a whole. Nonetheless, it pushed mankind up a few more percentage points on the Universe's "Species to keep an eye on" scale, and did at least get some forward thinking Travel Agents excitedly rubbing their hands together for about a week or so.

Mankind has built roads, bridges, ships, planes, trains, and automobiles, progressed from living in caves to cities, from running around in loin-clothes swinging big clubs, ripping up trees and communicating via grunts, to wearing Prada, hugging trees, and texting each other on mobile phones thus avoiding the need to directly communicate with each other at all.

We've invented electricity, the wheel, numbers, the compass, walked to the North and South Poles, created entire Empires, cured polio and smallpox, built pyramids, conceived of democracy, put a rather nice paint job on the ceiling of the Sistine chapel, and probably most importantly of all created beer, pizza, the push-up bra, and soccer.

These are all remarkable achievements that have changed our lives and the course of human history. There is much for Mr. and Mrs. Homo Sapiens to be proud of, and altogether not a bad list of achievements for a species that just a few million years ago was still climbing around in the trees eating bananas.

But for every amazing achievement there are hundreds of other examples where mankind has also fallen just a little short of such greatness, where attempts to conquer, invent, build, or overcome, have ended up more in red-faced embarrassment than glorious fist-pump.

Take for instance the Russians selling the giant landmass known as Alaska to the United States for about 2 cents an acre thinking it was just worthless tundra, but which actually turned out to be floating on a sea of oil and dollar bills. Or the Japanese choosing to mount a surprise attack on Pearl Harbour on December 7th 1941 hoping to cripple the U.S navy, only to turn up and find the largest Aircraft Carriers were not even in port that day. Or consider how the Persian leader who sent Genghis Khan's ambassador back to him minus his head felt when he woke up the next morning to find the might of the Mongol army banging on his front-door.

Or how about the next day red-faced blushes of the Decca Record executive who turned down the Beatles believing there was no market for a guitar group made up of incomprehensible scousers, the Safety Inspector who forgot to put back a safety valve on the Piper Alpha North Sea oil rig which directly led to an explosion killing 167 people and causing over $3bn of damage. Or how about the man who decided to fill the Hindenburg Airship with hydrogen gas rather than more expensive helium gas, which overnight turned the giant passenger carrying blimp into a giant fireball.

Sometimes, even what seems like the most insignificant wooden-headed act can go on to have rather unfortunate consequences on a global scale. Take for instance Archduke Franz Ferdinand's half-witted driver who on June 28th 1914 merely took a wrong turn down a Sarajevo street, and realizing his mistake decided to stop the car to turnaround, only to do so right in front of one of Ferdinand's would-be assassins, Gavrilo Princip, who had already given up on his mission and was on his way home for dinner, and now likely couldn't believe his own luck. The resulting impromptu assassination set off the chain of events that started World War I and the eventual death of millions, and all because Ferdinand's driver was probably reading his map upside down.

So here then is a collection of such knuckle-headed history-changing events, each driven by mistakes, bad decisions, bad luck, plain hollow-headed incompetence, or sometimes all four at once. There have of course been many other embarrassing moments throughout mankind's chequered history where reality didn't quite unfold the way the drawing-board blue-sky planning had pictured it, only further enhancing the argument that mankind is still very much an evolutionary work in progress. But what follows will at least give you a flavour of just what history changing incompetence mankind is capable of when our built-in, shock-proof, "maybe this isn't such a great idea after all" detector is inadvertently switched off, and we are just left with the unpredictable workings of the human brain.

French Retreat Due To Lack Of Turnips

Napoleon's disastrous attempt to invade Russia

Probably the last person you wanted to piss-off at the start of the 19th century was Napoleon Bonaparte. He had already run amuck across most of Europe winning a string of away-fixtures with his Grande Army of garlic eating Frenchies which had seen the self-appointed Emperor of all things French annex Belgium and Holland, along with large chunks of Italy and Croatia, set up dependencies in Switzerland, Poland and various German states, browbeat Austria, Prussia and Russia into becoming allies, and just for good measure forced everyone to drive on the wrong side of the road. It would have been the political equivalent of trying to French-kiss a shark.

It seems only the roast-beef and lager fuelled Brits remained completely outside of the grasp of the pint-sized leader who in response to their defiance had already ordered a full-scale Euro-wide embargo of any goods from the plucky Island nation, a blockade the likes of which would not be seen again until patriotic Americans were denied the joys of a good cigar when Uncle Sam had a small tiff with Fidel Castro.

However, in 1810 piss-off little "Boney" is exactly what Czar Alexander I of Russia did when he stopped complying with Bonaparte's anti-Brit embargo, a decision largely made due to its disastrous effect on Russian trade and thus the value of the rouble in his sizable pockets. And just in case Napoleon wasn't clear as to Russia's little change of heart, Alexander went on to also impose his own heavy tax on French luxury products such as garlic, onions, and berets, and in a clear attempt to avoid receiving wagon-loads of foul smelling French cheese every year for Christmas he even had the nerve to rebuff Napoleon's attempt to marry one of his sisters.

Clearly miffed, Napoleon jumped down from the booster-seat on his throne, stamped his feet a few times, and quickly moved to teach

Alexander a quick lesson in Napoleonic justice, vowing to quickly march on Russia, give Ivan a quick bloody nose to bring them back into line, and be back home comfortably sat on the Champs-Elysees drinking brandy and picking garlic from his teeth within a quick few months.

Generally regarded as one of history's top military tacticians Bonaparte's track record of military successes had been largely built on a method of warfare based on an ability to move his troops as fast as possible to the place they were needed the most, which military logic usually dictates to be a position roughly midway between your enemy and their objective.

Bonaparte recognized that the slowest part of any army at the time was the supply trains, and while a soldier could march 15 - 20 miles a day (a fact made even more impressive when you think how the French always stop for at least a two hour lunch-break), a supply wagon was generally limited to a snail-like 8 - 10 miles a day. Thus Napoleon insisted that his troops live as much as possible off the land, effectively feeding themselves as they went, moving like a swarm of locusts across the terrain. Great swathes of lowland Europe had already found its fields left empty of carrots, turnips, and onions as a result of Napoleon's wartime tactics.

However for such "eat-as-you-go" tactics to work, the terrain must co-operate. There must be a good road network for the army to quickly advance along, and a sufficient supply of suitable French stew ingredients conveniently lying around in the ground to sustain such a fast-moving mob of foraging hungry Frenchmen. But what in retrospect seems like a bit of a schoolboy error, no one it seems bothered to first check whether Russia would be just as accommodating in this respect as the rest of Europe had so far proved to be.

Regardless, not wanting to change what was clearly a winning formula, Napoleon duly amassed what was likely the largest European armed force ever assembled to that point (historians report upwards of 600,000 troops and over 50,000 horses) and planned to march headlong into Russia killing every Russian and eating every turnip they met up with on the way, and thus quickly forcing Alexander to see the error of his ways and bringing both him and his nation back in line with French foreign policy. The plan was simple and it had a proven track record of success, what could possibly go wrong?

Thus, on June 24th 1812, Napoleon led what probably looked like the entire male population of France across the Niemen River into Russia fully expecting to be home in time to enjoy a late Parisian summer. Unfortunately things would not quite work out as planned and started to go wrong almost as soon as Napoleon set foot on Russian soil.

Napoleon quickly discovered that Russian road-workers were clearly not of the same quality as those to be found across the rest of Europe, and found a Russian road network on a par with your average under-funded third-world nation, forcing him to advance over half a million troops along what was effectively just poorly constructed, pot-holed farm tracks. In addition to poor roads, the farmland turned out to be not quite the Smorgasbord of French cooking ingredients that was hoped for, and struggled just to feed the local population as it was let alone the sudden influx of half the population of France that Napoleon now expected to feed themselves by living off the land.

Consequently 600,000 hungry Frenchmen suddenly found themselves all using the same pot-holed tracks that passed for Russian roads while trying to feed themselves by foraging in fields whose prime bounty was weeds and rocks. This all resulted in the first troops at the head of the lengthy column feasting on what little food here was, but with subsequent sets of troops finding the cupboard somewhat bare, with those unfortunate enough to be bringing up the rear finding little or nothing with which to rustle-up their daily soup de jour.

The Russians made the problem worse by adopting a "fighting retreat" tactic pulling back and abandoning whole cities while setting fire to military stores and bridges on their way out and forcing peasants to burn what little their crops they had to prevent them from falling into French hands (or mouths). As time went by, soldiers began to straggle due to having to forage further and further away from the roads in search of their daily camembert and crackers, and Napoleon's well trained efficient fighting machine quickly became in danger of turning into more of an unruly, hungry mob of French speaking soccer hooligans suffering garlic withdrawal symptoms.

The situation was just as bad for the horses. What grazing there was to be found along the road was not adequate to maintain healthy horses, and the further the army went into Russia the less fodder was available. By the end of the first month, over 10,000 horses had already died, leaving an equal number of cavalrymen suddenly finding themselves equipped for battle on horseback but now having to adapt to a new life as foot-soldiers.

To make matters worse soldiers weakened by poor diets and fatigue quickly became susceptible to disease, and the poor food, combined with camping on sites where tens of thousands had bivouacked the night before (and thus contaminated the water and area with unwanted human waste) made diarrhoea and dysentery common. Things were starting to unravel for Napoleon very quickly and he hadn't even yet properly engaged with any significant Russian force who were all still busy keeping a safe distance ahead of him burning bridges and eating as many carrots and turnips as they could find to slow down, frustrate, and starve the rapidly dwindling French force.

The Russians did not truly make a stand until the September 7 Battle of Borodino, which took place just 75 miles from Moscow. French and Russian lines pounded each other with artillery and launched a number of charges and counter-charges, and losses on both sides were enormous, with total casualties of at least 70,000. Rather than continue with a second day of fighting, the Russian commanders took a collective "sod this for a way to make a living" decision and promptly withdrew leaving the road to Moscow open.

On September 14, Napoleon entered Moscow, only to find that most residents had already left the city, leaving behind vast quantities of vodka but little food. French troops subsequently drank themselves silly while Napoleon waited for Alexander to sue for peace, but no such offer ever came. With snow flurries having already fallen, Napoleon was left with little choice but to lead his army out of Moscow realizing that it could not survive the winter there.

By this time Napoleon was now down to some 100,000 troops, the rest having died, deserted, been wounded, captured, or left along the roadside still looking for ingredients to put in their woefully empty cooking pots. His troops were forced back along the same roads they took on the way to Moscow, but now all forage along that route had already been consumed. Meanwhile, men and horses continued to die in droves of starvation and disease, and the Grande Army's flanks and rear guard faced constant attacks from the Russian army's continuing sneaky guerrilla tactics.

To top it off, an unusually early and harsh winter quickly set in, complete with high winds, sub-zero temperatures and lots of snow. This was a bone-chilling cold that turned fingers (and worse) into popsicles, and where even the local peasants who were used to such conditions found it hard to survive let alone the "dressed for summer" French softies, and consequently thousands more men and horses succumbed to exposure.

By the time what was left of Napoleon's army had strapped tennis rackets on their feet and finally managed to walk back into Poland in early December, less than 100,000 exhausted, tattered Frenchmen remained of the 600,000 proud soldiers who had crossed the Niemen River some five months before. No one its seems even bothered to count the number of returning horses, if there were any at all.

Ultimately, Napoleon was undone by a lack of thermal underwear, disease, and poor Russian farming and infrastructure. He'd come to Russia looking for a quick head-to-head battle that would deliver a message, but found an enemy who didn't want to play using his version of the "how to wage a war" rule book, and he returned to France with his pantaloons firmly down around his ankles, chastened, and significantly lighter on the troops front. It was a significant blow to Napoleon's "small man" syndrome, and to France as a whole.

The retreat from Russia proved to be the beginning of the end for Napoleon, as emboldened by the sight of Napoleon limping back to Paris with his tail firmly between his short little legs, Austria, Prussia and Sweden decided to finally grow a pair and re-joined Russia and Great Britain in the fight against him. Although the French Emperor was able to raise another army, it was a little short on both cavalry and experience, and consequently Napoleon suffered yet another crushing defeat in October 1813 at the Battle of Leipzig, and by the following March, Paris had been captured and Napoleon was duly frog-marched into exile on the island of Elba.

However, clearly not one to accept defeat gracefully Napoleon made one more great attempt to re-take power. After escaping Elba and raising yet another army, he was finally overcome at the Battle of Waterloo in 1815 by the Duke of Wellington, and thus ensuring a later Eurovision song contest win for Sweden. This time Napoleon was sent to the remote island of Saint Helena in the middle of the Atlantic ocean from where even Houdini would have found it hard to escape, and where the once ruler of most of Europe lived out his final days likely wishing he'd never bothered with Russia at all.

Note to anyone planning an invasion of Russia: don't forget to take woolly socks and a packed-lunch.

Bird War I

The Australian Army declares war on the mighty emu

The Australian armed forces have earned a reputation for bravery, valour, and honour in just about every conflict they have willingly participated in. They are famed for beating off enemies with nothing more than a cricket bat, a rolled up copy of Barbeque Weekly, and a fly-swat. Gallipoli, Tobruk, El Alamein, Passchendaele, all demonstrated that although unfortunately usually returning home somewhat fewer in number, your average plucky Mel Gibson-type always stepped off the boat in Sydney harbour with a cold-one in their hand and with their heads held high having seen off whatever or whoever had upset their Aussie sensitivities.

However, during the somewhat quieter years between World War I and the rather unimaginatively named subsequent World War II, the reputation of the Aussie fighting machine was to face its toughest test.

Following World War I, large numbers of Australian ex-soldiers had taken up wheat and livestock farming in Western Australia lured by cheap land and the promise of Government subsidies, and probably as it was seen as a somewhat safer alternative to some of the other options on offer down at the local job-centre at the time such as crocodile wrestling, or convincing sharks to kindly stay away from public beaches.

However, in 1932, likely drawn by the acres of fresh new wheat to eat, the conveniently placed watering holes that had been made available for livestock, and also likely fed up with listening to Aborigines playing their didgeridoos around Ayers rock, the farmers suddenly found their lands overrun by tens of thousands of migrating emus.

Now the emu is not your average sweet singing, build a nest in the trees, Sunday lunch for cats, kind of bird. The average emu weighs in at around 100lbs, stands six feet tall, is highly intelligent, and stronger than a bull on steroids. Given their size, weight, and lack of Boeing jet engines it's no surprise that they can't fly, but make up for their lack of vertical lift with a running speed of over 30 miles per hour. They are 2-legged, highly aggressive, eating machines that should not be taken lightly. If emus were men they'd probably all be Scottish, and you certainly wouldn't want your daughter marrying one of them. Needless to say that within days of their arrival the army of emus were ransacking crops, tearing down fences and turning watering holes into just mere holes.

To make matters worse such fearsome birds were never likely to be scared off by some less than intimidating farmer look-a-likes made of straw strategically placed in the middle of fields, and dressed in Grandma's old hat old and clothes, and with their long necks seemingly made of rubber they were easily able to avoid all attempts to stop them in their tracks with the Aussie weapon of choice, the boomerang.

The farmers of Western Australia recognized they clearly needed help, and a delegation was swiftly dispatched to Canberra to meet with the Minister of Defence, where they requested help from the government to fight the growing emu menace.

Having actively served in World War I the soldiers-cum-farmers had faced many enemies, and they knew that men with sticks making loud shooing noises was never going to work against such a foe. No, what was needed was guns, and not just any old guns, the farmers insisted on full-on, rapid-fire, machine-guns. The minister relented. He would send the weapons, but not trusting that the farmers wouldn't just run amok across Western Australia firing off automatic weapons at anything roughly 6 foot tall that looked like it couldn't fly, he also stipulated that he would also send active serving soldiers to man the guns.

The eradication of the emu was thus to be an official text-book military operation, and the ministry ordered no less than Major G.P.W. Meredith, Commander of the Royal Australian Artillery's Seventh Heavy Battery, to lead the mission. War was officially declared, sweethearts kissed their brave soldiers goodbye, radio broadcasts were made wishing the plucky troops a speedy return home from the front, and within days Major Meredith found himself in the strange and unforgiving land known as Western Australia, leading battle-hardened soldiers, complete with some big-ass heavy machine guns, and ready to unleash hell on a bunch of seemingly helpless birds. The Great Emu War of 1932 had begun.

Meredith planned to quickly annihilate the emus with two Lewis machine guns and a stockpile of 10,000 rounds of ammunition and be back home before the first Red-Cross parcels had arrived. The Lewis is a gas-operated American weapon that was used extensively during World War I, and which could fire 500 rounds of ammunition per minute, and thus the soldiers, both current and former, were confident the birds would be either dead or chased back to Ayers rock within a matter of days. The emus as it turned out clearly had other ideas.

The official campaign was due to begin in October 1932, however, the operation was delayed by a period of heavy rainfall which caused the emus to scatter over a much wider area, and forced Meredith to send back requests to Canberra for raincoats and some somewhat broader maps of Western Australia.

However, the rain ceased by early November, at which point the troops were deployed with orders to "unleash hell" on the unsuspecting emus, and according to newspaper accounts, as an added bonus they were to collect at least 1,000 emu skins so that their feathers could be used to add a touch of flair to the hats of the recognized poster-boys of the Australian military, the Australian Light Horse Brigade who had their annual group photo-shoot planned shortly.

However, the very first engagement of the operation merely proved that the emus were surprisingly gifted in the art of guerrilla warfare, something Meredith was presumably made unaware of at his mission briefing. Herding the emus together for easy pickings proved near impossible, and they scattered in every direction the second the first bullets flew. Only a handful of birds succumbed to the initial hail of bullets unleashed by Meredith's troops, with most vanishing into the bush leaving the soldiers with nothing remotely bird-like to aim at.

Meredith regrouped, quickly consulted his standard issue Military Tactics Handbook, and decided that the best plan of attack under the circumstances would be to set up a proper military ambush in order to surprise the emus. By the morning of the 4th of November Meredith had duly established a text-book ambush near a local dam. The troops waited silently, and eventually an unsuspecting battalion of over 1,000 emus were spotted heading towards their position.

This time the gunners waited until the birds were in close proximity before opening fire. However, unfortunately one of the guns jammed after only twelve birds had been killed, and the remainder once again scattered before any more could be killed. No emus were ever sighted at the dam again.

Now running out of options in his tactical playbook, Meredith's frustration reached critical levels. Thus, ignoring all recognized formal rules of engagement and military etiquette, he resorted to mounting one of the machine guns on the back of a truck in order to just flat out drive-by mow-down the giant birds.

However, the emus easily outran the truck leading it over such rough terrain that the gunner didn't even manage to get off a single shot. The chase was brought to an abrupt and red-faced end when the truck crashed through a fence. Meredith, his driver, and the gunner were forced to walk back to base carrying both the Lewis machine gun and their full complement of bullets. The full complement of emus merely stopped for lunch at the next available wheat field.

By the 8th of November, six days into the military campaign, over 2,500 rounds of ammunition had been fired with just 50 confirmed emu kills. However, on the plus side Meredith's official report later proudly noted that his men had themselves suffered no casualties, that is other than one badly damaged truck, one copy of the Australian Army Field Manual which had been found torn-up by "personnel unknown", and some slightly red-faces. Perhaps in his own defence, Meredith also commented upon the "emu's striking manoeuvrability, even while badly wounded" stating that "if we had a military division with the bullet-carrying capacity of these birds it would face any army in the world. They can face machine guns with the invulnerability of tanks".

Having had their share of humiliation, the crest-fallen soldiers had no option but to admit defeat after just one week in the field, and with heads bowed they skulked back to Canberra.

After the withdrawal of the military, the emu attacks on crops continued unabated. Farmers again asked Canberra for support, citing that the hot weather and drought that was drawing emus in their thousands to wreak havoc on their farmland, and this time even the Premier of Western Australia lent his strong support and if pictures are to be believed also his considerable weight for the resumption of military action.

By the 12th of November the Minister of Defence had approved a resumption of military efforts, and so with much trepidation Maj. G.P.W. Meredith and the Royal Australian Artillery's Seventh Heavy Battery were once again placed in the field to do battle with the ever growing emu army.

Taking to the field on 13 November 1932, Meredith this time found a degree of success with approximately 40 emus killed in the first two days of combat. However, the third day, 15 November, proved to be far less successful, but by 2 December the guns were apparently accounting for approximately 100 emus per week.

This time Meredith sent back glowing reports to Canberra about the devastation he had rained down on the enemy ranks. According to Meredith, close to 1,000 emus had been killed after his men had fired off all their ammunition, and claiming that an additional 2,500 more had succumbed to their injuries after taking hostile fire. These claims were of course impossible to verify, and it's entirely possible that Meredith inflated his own numbers to save face, and likely his military career.

However, it was abundantly clear to the Australian parliament that the emus had won, and that Meredith's two campaigns had ultimately been entirely ineffective. At the beginning of December Meredith, his men, and the Lewis machine guns were once again called back east, leaving the farmers to fend for themselves against the emu threat.

Parliament, likely noting the reams of bad press and embarrassing lack of dead emus, withdrew all military support and spending from the Emu War, and officially declared the hostilities over. However, this ceasefire was never officially communicated to the emus, who likely still believe the war is in progress even today.

Scots Make Schoolboy Error, Twice

Scotland invades England during the midst of a Plague

In the spring of 1348 a merchant ship from the Far East sailed into Sicily with its cargo of silk, spices, and several crates full of fake handbags and watches. In addition to its manifested cargo, the ship also brought with it some unwanted passengers in the shape of black rats, who themselves were unsuspecting carriers of fleas carrying a disease that would unfortunately go on to wipe out about 25 million unsuspecting Europeans over the course of the next 3 years, that's about half the population of Europe at the time. The disease was the bubonic plague.

At the time theories about the cause of the disease were numerous, ranging from a punishment from God, to unfortunate planetary alignment, to the evil stares from upset neighbors. Not surprisingly, many people believed that the horrors of the plague signaled the coming of the Apocalypse, others believed that the disease was actually a plot by Jews to poison all of the Christian world, a theory that saw many Jews killed by panicked mobs long before the disease they were supposed to have concocted got them anyway.

By the time the flea covered rats were identified as the root cause it was already too late, even the Pied Piper of Hamelin could not have saved Europe. Rats have suffered a bad rap in Europe ever since, although truth be told it was the fleas that were the primary instigators, they just set the rats up to take the fall.

The bubonic plague is a bacteria-born disease, the bacteria was carried in the blood of wild rats and the fleas that lived off them. Normally there is no contact between these fleas and human beings, but when their rat hosts eventually died, these needy little fleas seek out suitable alternatives, and the next most accessible host in Europe around that time was the rapidly growing urban populations of human beings.

The disease itself came on rapidly in those unfortunate enough to be caught in the way of its steady march across Europe, producing several symptoms in its victims ranging from intense headaches, to high temperatures, and Olympic standard projectile vomiting. It also caused very painful fist-sized swellings, usually around the groin, armpits or neck, which oozed pus and were black in colour giving the disease its more commonly known name, the "Black Death". The infected, perhaps mercifully, were usually dead within the week, although the few that did manage to survive the disease found themselves very quickly off everyone's Christmas card list.

It isn't clear exactly when or where the Black Death eventually reached England, some reports pointed to Bristol, others to Dorset, and appearing as early as June 1348. But once landed the disease spread through England with dizzying speed. The effect was worse in the cities where overcrowding and primitive sanitation meant that the plague infested fleas could jump from human to human without having to break into too much of a sweat at all, and by November 1348 the Black Death had reached London, ruining Christmas and severely reducing the number of New year's eve parties. Over the next 2 years the disease killed about 40% of the entire population of England, that's about 2 million people who suffered a very painful death in England alone.

Now maybe rats just don't like porridge or seeing men not wearing any underpants, but strangely (at first at least) the plague did not cross Hadrian's wall into Scotland at all, and the Scots remained blissfully free, and largely ignorant, of the unpleasant epidemic that was happening just south of their doorstep.

When the Scots did eventually hear that the "old enemy" were being ravaged by a highly infectious disease they were of course absolutely delighted. It had been over 30 years since Robert the Bruce had scored Scotland's greatest home win against England at the Battle of Bannockburn in 1314, when the then rather effeminate (allegedly) King of England, Edward II, was sent back south to his embroidery and his "man-friend" Piers Gaveston (allegedly), with his tail between his legs. But since then they had suffered a series of humiliating defeats at the hands of the new and rather more butch-like King, Edward III, and so anything that undermined the English was seen as a wholly positive thing and so naturally something to be celebrated.

Now in what turned out to be one of the less impressive pieces of Scottish intellectual reasoning, the Scots managed to convince themselves that the disease was the "revenging hand of God" against the much hated English (seems they conveniently ignored the reports of the disease also ravaging most of continental Europe) and so they naturally also assumed that the Scots themselves were immune to such a "holy" disease.

It was then only just a matter of time until someone had what must have seemed like a bright idea at the time. Wouldn't this be the perfect time to invade England, after all the English were now all either dead, in the process of becoming dead, or busy mourning or clearing up after the dead?

Now this kind of thinking was probably not the product of a particularly balanced mind, but regardless a vote was taken and unanimously passed by some very senior ginger bearded men in skirts, and by the autumn of 1349 Scotland's finest had assembled in Selkirk forest with the single-minded intention of invading England.

And so, after downing several man-sized bowls of porridge to sustain them on their quest, and letting out a pre-departure rallying cry of "Freedom!" in their best Mel Gibson impersonations, the Scottish troops marched south to raid the English city of Durham intent on letting what remaining English they found taste some well tempered Scottish steel. Up to this point no one seems to have spotted the obvious flaw in their bold invasion plan, but, once across the border it was not too long before the penny dropped for the tartan-kilted army.

Having avoided the ravages of the Black Death up to this point primarily by avoiding any direct contact with either the offending rats, fleas, or infected Englishmen, the initially buoyant Scottish troops soon found that south of the border they too were now starting to breakout in painful black swellings, vomiting large quantities of yesterday's porridge, and complaining of headaches.

Within a couple of weeks of marching south over 5,000 Scots had perished at the hands of the Black Death. However, now having realized their mistake the rapidly depleting Scottish invasion force now made an even bigger one. They decided to pack up and go home.

What was now left of the Scottish troops now rather embarrassingly marched back into Scotland, home to their wives, children, and friends, and carrying with them the infectious disease. Within a year, more than a quarter of the population of Scotland was dead, killed by the Black Death and some rather poorly thought out military strategy.

Now if the Scots had had something other than cold porridge between their ears they probably would have realized that all they really needed to do was just wait, stay safely behind the giant flea barrier that was Hadrian's wall, let the plague do all the dirty work for them by killing most, if not all, the English, then when it was safe just march straight down to London, rename it McLondon, force everyone to eat haggis for dinner and porridge for breakfast, and thus claim England for themselves with little or no resistance. Alas, this plan was apparently never discussed, and thus the year 1349 was to become a year that Scottish historians try very hard to forget.

"Where The Hell Did That Iceberg Come From?"

The Titanic forgets it's unsinkable

On 10 April 1912 the most famous ship ever built left Southampton harbour on its maiden voyage. It carried on board 2,200 passenger and crew, 20,000 bottles of beer, 1,500 bottles of wine 8,000 cigars, several of the world's richest people, along with movie stars Leonardo DiCaprio and Kate Winslet, all bound for New York. The ship was the RMS Titanic.

When it was launched the *Titanic* was the largest ship afloat. For those impressed by numbers she was 882.5 feet long, 92.5 feet wide, and 175 feet high, which is roughly the size of the Empire State building lying on its side, and at the time it was the largest man-made moving object on planet Earth. Several other much larger man-made objects such as numerous bridges, buildings, and dams had in theory "moved" when they unfortunately collapsed or toppled over, but as this was never part of their initial purpose they can be discounted.

In addition to its size, the Titanic was also designed to be the ultimate in luxury travel. Never had a cruise ship had such magnificent features, apparently inspired by the Ritz hotel in London, it including a gymnasium, swimming pool, libraries, restaurants, luxurious cabins (at least in 1st class), a Turkish bath, a kennel for first class dogs, and in a new high point in cruise ship luxury it even had communal baths for the 3rd class passengers.

Not content with the glossy holiday brochures proudly detailing the biggest, fastest, most luxurious liner in the known universe, in a rather bold piece of marketing the White Star Line's owners also put down their fat cigars just long enough to proudly claim that as an added bonus the Titanic was also "unsinkable". However, after a brief consultation with their lawyers possibly concerned about potential future lawsuits, the bold claim was actually down-graded to state that she was in fact "practically unsinkable", close enough, but nevertheless still a brave act of bravado given that the Universe rarely takes kindly to such bold claims.

It came as no big surprise then for those more attuned to the karmic ways of the Universe that within 4 days of leaving Southampton, the Titanic had found itself a new permanent home at the bottom of the Atlantic ocean.

Actually, alarm bells should have already have been ringing in the ears of any potential passengers who rather than believe the hype actually bothered to dig a little deeper into the bold claims coming from the White Star Line Boardroom.

Firstly, a quick look at the small print would have shown that the Captain of this mighty beast on its maiden voyage was to be one Captain E. J. Smith on what was also to be his last command prior to retiring from the White Star line to settle down to a life of playing Battleships in his bathtub and polishing his medals.

A cursory scan of Captain Smith's resume would have alerted them to the fact that by now he was already 68 years old and likely with his mind half on his Florida retirement home, and more worryingly with something of past record of denting his driver's no-claims bonus with a history of hitting other sizable objects in the path of the ships under his command. In 1911 alone Smith had somehow managed to run over one of the tugs assisting in the docking of the RMS Olympic under his command in New York Harbour, and a few months later had collided with the British warship HMS Hawke damaging her bow. If any Captain of the White Star Line was going to hit something, the smart money was always on Captain E. J. Smith.

In addition, any passenger with even the slightest engineering background would have noticed that the whole ship looked like it was being held together by sub-standard iron rivets, about 3 million of them, all of which would not hold up to a good kick let alone any substantial impact. Titanic it seems was effectively just held together by sticky tape and glue. For what was at the time the largest ocean-going vessel in the known universe, it was seemingly built not much better than a kid's model airplane.

Probably of greater concern however would have been the lifeboat situation on the ship. Had the crew of the Titanic bothered to hold a lifeboat drill (likely they were all too busy trying to get Leonardo DiCaprio's autograph) passengers would have noticed that there were actually only 16 wooden lifeboats and four collapsible lifeboats onboard, barely enough to carry around 1,200 people. However, with 2,200 passengers and crew onboard even the most mathematically challenged of the passengers should have been able to figure out that this might pose something of a problem if Captain Smith continued his current driving form.

For such a ship where seemingly no expense was spared, the decision to carry only half the number of needed lifeboats seems a bit of a glaring oversight, particularly given that looking back over nautical history it's hard to find any mitigating example where the Captain of a ship had ever given the order to "half abandon ship", or where a ship had only "half" sunk. At the last minute someone did suggest that they stock one of the store rooms with some pedelos and a few dozen inflatable lilos just in case, but this idea seems to have been ignored.

Regardless of these initial warning signs, after brief stops in Cherbourg in France and Queenstown in Ireland, Captain Smith pointed the Titanic and its 2,200 passengers and crew in the general direction of west and headed off for New York.

For the next few days everything went well. The 1st class passengers enjoyed their champagne, cigars, and silver-service 10 course meals, and the 3rd class passengers all happily huddled together to keep warm several decks below well out of sight of the other passengers and crew.

Despite receiving several warnings of icebergs making their way south and into the shipping lanes, and more importantly likely on a collision course with the Titanic, Captain Smith kept his foot firmly on the accelerator pedal, pushing at full speed towards the waiting Statue of Liberty, the opportunity for a potential 6 day record breaking Atlantic crossing, and the beckoning call of his retirement pipe and slippers.

It appears that the Titanic did actually received 6 iceberg warnings, but Captain Smith had his eyes firmly on the prize, he duly posted lookouts to keep an eye out for any large white floating objects that might drift across Titanic's unwavering path, but continued to throw all incoming iceberg warnings in the bin, pushed on full-steam ahead, and continued to read his book on the top 10 things to do in Florida.

At 11:40pm on April 14, lookout Fredrick Fleet suddenly realised he was rapidly coming face to face with a more than sizable looking iceberg that was quietly bobbing around in the water right in the path of the fully-stoked Titanic. Before Fleet even had time to fire off a few choice expletives the Titanic had hit the iceberg, the glancing blow meeting little resistance from the putty-like rivets and causing a tear in the ship's hull about the length of 2 football fields down its right side. Within seconds the Titanic was fast turning into a giant bucket of sea water.

Many accusing eyes were subsequently turned on those assigned to lookout for such sizable floating objects, and as to why they only saw the iceberg 30 seconds before the Titanic turned into a 50,000 tonne battering ram, after all, the iceberg was reportedly about 100 foot high and 400 foot long, it was no ice-cube, it was basically the size of the Colosseum in Rome, and as such presumably should not have been that hard to miss.

In their defence however, it seems that the role of lookout was not deemed important enough by those safely sat drinking hot chocolate in the warmth of the Bridge to bother to unlock the binoculars from their safe storage and hand them out to those whose job was to look out to the distant horizon for any such blocks of ice the size of Italian landmarks. But even without the advantage binoculars, it's still hard to imagine that they could miss seeing a full-scale floating ice-sculpture of the Colosseum until 30 seconds before it was on top of them.

The belief that the Titanic was unsinkable was, in part, due to the fact that the she had been constructed with what was considered at the time the revolutionary idea of having sixteen watertight compartments along its length. The theory being that even if 4 of the 16 compartments were breached the ship would still remain afloat.

Unfortunately, as it turns out, icebergs are no respecters of engineering drawings or revolutionary design concepts, and the gash this particular iceberg inflicted was long enough to ensure that 6 compartments would quickly become giant fish tanks. A quick review of the Titanic's owner's manual quickly advised that the allegedly "unsinkable" ship was now not only going to sink, but it was going to do so rather quickly. In fact, the Titanic was doomed to a watery grave from the second the iceberg struck, just that no one had quite realized it just yet.

Things were already now looking less than rosy for the Titanic but the universe continued to do its rain-dance, and what followed next can best be described as nothing short of farcical. It was more than a hour after the collision with the iceberg before anyone in authority even deemed the situation bad enough to issue the order to abandon ship, by which time the ship was already well on its way to turning submarine. In the less than an hour and half that would remain before the Titanic finally gave in to gravity, disorganized and chaotic scenes broke out that would make any Black Friday Sale look like a village church fete as the process of evacuation and the lowering of the lifeboats began.

Not only were there not enough lifeboats to save everyone on board, but in the panic and chaos most of the lifeboats were launched half empty. Despite being designed to hold up to 65 people, the first lifeboat left with only 24 people aboard, with 1 lifeboat actually launching with only 7 crew and 5 passengers onboard, although these passengers did later give full marks on the post-cruise survey for the greater than one-to-one crew to passenger service they unexpectedly received.

Some 1st class passengers merely resigned themselves to their fate, changed into their formal evening wear and were last spotted on deck-chairs drinking brandy and smoking cigars as the ship went under, while others apparently refused to even get into the lifeboats at all until they had been suitably stocked with wine, cheese, and cigars.

Realizing that time, and indeed the number of lifeboats, was quickly running out many others just jumped from the deck into the icy waters over 100 feet below in a vain attempt to save themselves. However, untrained in high-board diving this merely resulted in the last act of many being an impressive but terminal belly-flop, while with the sea temperature being a less than inviting minus 2 degrees centigrade those brave souls that did survive the jump lasted less than 20 minutes before turning blue and ending their days as fish food.

Back onboard, following in the long showbiz tradition of "the show must go on", the ship's band did its best to keep up morale by continuing to play for passengers while the chaos of abandoning ship continued on around them, possibly just happy to have the opportunity to play something other than just endless requests for "My heart will go on", although playing bagpipe music might well have helped speed along the evacuation.

The ship finally broke in 2 at around 2.20am on April 15, and headed for the nearest solid land which was unfortunately 2 miles straight down. It had only been 160 minutes from the time the Titanic hit the iceberg to the time it finally sank beneath the waves taking with it over 1,500 of its passengers and crew, including Captain E. J. Smith who, dutifully following the unwritten law of the sea, went down with his ship. We can only assume that despite his recent track record, Captain Smith managed to guide the Titanic to its final resting place without hitting anything else on the way down.

The first ship that actually bothered to answer Titanic's distress calls was the RMS Carpathia which was more than 50 miles and 3 hours away. When it finally arrived it found only 705 survivors in half filled lifeboats and some floating debris where it had fully expected to find something more resembling the world's largest passenger liner.

In a further tragic twist, subsequent inquiries into the cause of the disaster noted that the final iceberg warning sent to the Titanic had been sent from a ship much closer by, the SS Californian, captained by Stanley Lord, which had stopped for the night less than a cross-channel swim away from Titanic's position. However, it seems that at around 11.15pm the Californian's radio operator deciding that his shift was over for the day, turned off the radio and went to bed for the night and thus the Titanic's "Ooops, we've just hit an iceberg, please come help" pleas over the radio remained unheard. Although the discovery of the remains of the Titanic on the sea bed, in 1985, makes it clear that the S.O.S position given was itself off by 13 miles anyway.

To make matters worse, it appears that sometime after midnight the crew on watch of the Californian reported seeing rockets being fired into the sky on the horizon. Captain Lord was informed but rather than interpret them as the Titanic sending distress signals, he merely concluded that the ship was clearly having a something of a wild party, took no action, and went back to bed.

Looking for an easy target to pin the huge loss of life on the subsequent inquiries into the disaster made Captain Lord something of a scapegoat for his lack of response to Titanic's frantic pleas. He was subsequently fired by his employers and presumably spent the rest of his days dressed in heavy disguise hiding from angry Titanic survivors.

Basic lessons were clearly learned from the disaster. Going forward all ships would at least give the appearance of having enough lifeboats for all passengers and crew, lifeboat drills themselves became mandatory if for nothing else than as a way to confirm that there were indeed enough lifeboats to go round. Ships radios were now to be manned 24 hours a day, speed limit signs went up all over the Atlantic, mandatory eye tests were introduced for ship's lookouts, and basic "This is what an iceberg looks like" training was introduced for all ship's crew. Marketing Companies also removed the word "unsinkable" from all their training manuals.

However, on the positive side, Kate Winslet was identified as one of the 705 survivors, and the whole story would go on to win 11 Academy awards. The Board of the White Star Line would have been proud.

Houston We Have A Problem

Simple math error destroys NASA Mars Orbiter

Getting a rocket into space is not as easy as just strapping some big-ass engines to the back of a your dad's Ford Escort, pointing it skyward, counting down from 10, turning the ignition, and watching as the whole thing gracefully propels itself toward the stars. It's also a task made substantially more difficult if you want to strap on some willing astronauts to tag along for the ride, and doubly so if your plans in any way include bringing them back home again alive.

Firstly, your rocket needs to leave the safety of the launch-pad and reach a speed of at least 25,000mph in just a matter of minutes to ensure that it can break free of the Earth's gravitational pull, which alone requires both some seriously large engines and a very large quantity of some very explosive and very expensive fuel.

Once outside of the Earth's atmosphere you need to cater for the zero-gravity of space where the earthly laws of physics just don't apply, and coming back is just as troublesome, as the friction generated between the air and your now rapidly falling tin-can as it re-enters back into the Earth's atmosphere heats its outer shell to temperatures of up to 1,250 degrees centigrade.

Then of course you need some way to rapidly slow your craft down enough to safely land it back on the ground without creating a sizable rocket-shaped crater. This all takes a bit of serious thinking about, and of course a great deal of money.

It's also not all just about taking in the views and pushing the odd button every now and again when the current occupation on your Driver's Licence states "Astronaut". Flying into outer-space squeezed inside a small tin-can that sits on top of a veritable ocean of rocket fuel is no picnic and not for the faint-hearted.

Up in space there are no flushing toilets, your drinking water is recycled pee, constantly living under zero-gravity means that your muscles waste away, your eyesight deteriorates, and you suffer almost constant motion sickness, while every time you put something down it frustratingly floats off, and to top it all off the suits they make you wear are hardly flattering either. Add to this the almost constant threat that something rather catastrophic could happen at any time rendering you either fried, frozen, crushed, asphyxiated, or heading off for an unscheduled meeting with the sun, and it's not too hard to see why one of the prime pre-requisites for being an astronaut is to have balls made of titanium.

The front-runners in the space-race have always been the U.S and Russia. Others have made attempts at reaching for the stars but have generally failed due to a combination of under-funding and having their best players poached by the significantly more attractive employment terms offered by the two previously mentioned premier league clubs.

Thus, despite several valiant attempts, the British Space program has yet to see a launch clear the local tree-line let alone the Earth's gravity, the French Space program has stalled apparently due to disagreements over the in-flight wine list, while there are unconfirmed reports that the North Korean Space program abruptly ended when the 3 astronauts manning the program's inaugural flight unexpectedly changed course immediately after clearing North Korean airspace and headed straight for Europe to seek political asylum. The space programs of most other countries don't seem to have got much beyond watching re-runs of Star Trek and so are unlikely to trouble the infinite void of space anytime soon.

In fact it was the Russians who first managed to get a human into orbit and back again in one piece. Although Yuri Gagarin was hailed as a hero around the world after becoming the first man to complete an orbit of the Earth in his Vostok spacecraft on 12th April 1961, the Russians had first taken the precaution of already testing the water the previous year by sending up 2 dogs, Belka and Strelka, onboard the Sputnik 5 spacecraft. However, on their safe return to Earth Belka and Strelka were greeted with rather less fanfare than Gagarin would later receive, and as to what state the two of them had left the inside of their spacecraft in has never been made public.

But such successes were always shrouded by suspicions that in their pursuit to be the first into space the Russians kept hidden from the world the fact that their spacecraft seem to have been nothing more than just second-hand tractors with large rockets strapped to the sides, which alongside their seemingly complete disregard for any levels of safety, meant that between the well publicized success stories there were likely many more rather less than well publicized failures.

Take for instance the Soyuz 23 spacecraft with her crew of 2 cosmonauts, which launched on October 16, 1976, bound toward the Russian Space-station Salyut 5. The omens did not look good for the mission from the start when the bus transporting the 2 cosmonauts broke down on the way to the launch-pad causing a delay while they presumably waited for a mechanic from the local village to come out and fix it. Meanwhile, someone also clearly forgot to check the daily weather report as shortly after its eventual liftoff the craft began to veer dangerously off-course due to heavy winds, requiring some frantic recalculations back at mission control and the two cosmonauts wishing they'd brought along a change of underwear.

Once finally in orbit, Soyuz 23 tried docking with Salyut 5 as planned, but the docking program somehow malfunctioned and rather than move them gently towards the Space-station it kept sending them away in the opposite direction. After numerous failed attempts to correct the error, and with fuel now running low, the ground-control crew eventually just gave up all together and ordered the cosmonauts to simply turn around and come back home.

However, the problems for the two hapless cosmonauts were not over yet. The Soyuz was supposed to land in Arkalyk, Kazakhstan, but yet more vicious winds pushed it to an icy lake over 75 miles away. After touchdown, the parachute used to slow the craft's descent began taking on water, dragging the spacecraft deeper into the lake. The cosmonauts had to wait till morning when the rescue party finally arrived and tried to lift the module from the water, but the rescue helicopter just wasn't strong enough, so they had to resort to simply dragging the capsule to shore instead. Eleven hours after Soyuz 23 touched down, it finally reached the safety of dry land. To the surprise of the rescue crew, both cosmonauts emerged safe and well, but both were seemingly demanding answers to what appeared to be some rather pressing questions.

But even the Russian's with their cut-price hardware and cavalier approach to safety would find it hard to beat the levels of just good old plain incompetence demonstrated by NASA when it tried to put an interplanetary weather satellite into orbit around Mars.

NASA's Mars Climate Orbiter mission began in December 1998 when a $125M rocket carrying a state of the art weather satellite was pointed in the general direction of Mars and launched from Cape Canaveral on a journey that was expected to take it about 9 months to reach its final destination.

Now much to the disappointment of early space scientists it seems that you can't just point your spacecraft towards Mars, let it go, and then all go on holiday for the next several months trusting that it will arrive at the red planet roughly when you expected it to, at which point you just reassemble the team back on Earth and get back to work.

Given that Mars is around 50 million miles away from Earth, it seems that any slight variation from its planned path could easily see the Orbiter ultimately miss Mars altogether, which would throw something of a spanner in the works in the overall mission plans, and so the clever navigation bods back at Mission-control have to constantly monitor its flight path, making small adjustments along the way to ensure it stays on course.

Now the process to make all this happen is relatively straightforward, in rocket-science terms anyway. A thingamajig on the Orbiter sends details of its current position to a thingamebob back at Mission-control, where the clever navigation bods then calculate the Orbiter's current path and make any needed adjustments to its trajectory by sending back messages to a different thingamajig on the Orbiter, that then fires its thrusters just enough to get it back on track. All quite simple really.

However, unbeknown to the bods sat at Mission-control there was a problem with all this measuring and readjusting that was going on. It seems that the computer software happily sending and receiving data on the Orbiter had been built to NASA's rigid specifications that meant that all measurements, including the impulse messages telling the thrusters how much to fire, were all being done in metric. While back at Mission-control, the computer software which calculated the total impulse produced by thruster firings, which had been out-sourced to Lockheed Martin and who were clearly all away on an office team-building exercise the day the email was sent about the Metric standard for all computer software, was happily producing its own calculations in Imperial measurements. So Metric onboard the spacecraft, Imperial on the ground, and no one it seemed to have a clue.

Now what all this means is that although Mission-control and the Orbiter were seeing the same numbers, the Orbiter was translating the numbers into a somewhat smaller metric-based blasts on the thrusters than the software back on Earth had calculated. The navigational bods were noticing that they were strangely having to make far more adjustments to the Orbiter's trajectory than they had expected, but no one raised any alarms seemingly just happy with all the extra overtime pay.

Amazingly, after nine and half months of incorrect adjustments to its flight path, the Orbiter still somehow made it to Mars in September of 1999, its arrival it seems more due to luck than judgement. Having all patted themselves on the back for getting their shiny Orbiter to Mars in one piece, the team at Mission-control then gathered themselves ready to put it into orbit around Mars ready to begin its daily weather reports from the red planet.

However, all those incorrect minor adjustments had taken their toll, as soon as Mission-control fired the Orbiter's main engines to supposedly put it into orbit around Mars they promptly lost all contact with it. NASA spent the next few days sitting around scratching their heads and pointing fingers, but they had no idea just what had happened to their $125M Mars Climate Orbiter.

Finally, a hastily convened "Mishap Investigation Board" (yes, NASA actually has such things) unearthed the unfortunate disconnect between the two systems used for the engine impulse measurements. It seems that at the point Mission-control fired the main engines to supposedly gracefully place the Orbiter into orbit, the spacecraft was actually over 100 miles closer to Mars than their calculations were telling them, and way too close to achieve any such manoeuvre successfully.

After over 9 months travelling to get to Mars, the Mars Climate Orbiter, along with its Metric calculating computer software, just headed straight for the surface of Mars and burnt up. While all along NASA was under the impression it was gently guiding a state of the art weather satellite to Mars, in reality all it had done was fire a $125M cannon-ball straight at the red-planet.

The loss of a $125M piece of hardware was embarrassing enough, but to do so because no one had bothered to check that all the computer systems were actually using the same type of measurements before they sent it all skyward highlighted a level of negligence that was hard to cover up with technical jargon and excuses, after all, it's not rocket science, well actually in this particular case it was, but you know what I mean. It was like filling your petrol-driven car with diesel or taking a French-English dictionary on your trip to Spain, a red-faced NASA had learned a very expensive lesson in very basic math.

Russia of course never suffered any such issues with their spacecraft, they just never bothered with any such expensive hi-tech computers, all such calculations were done by hand on a scrap of paper, after all, nothing had ever gone wrong with a Russian space mission anyway.

Kublai Khan Loses Two-Leg Fixture Against Japan

The Mongol Invasions of Japan

Between 1206 and his death in 1227, a span of just 25 years, Genghis Khan and his Mongol hoards managed to conquer nearly 12 million square miles of territory, an area larger than the Romans had managed over the course of four centuries, and more than any other individual in history. Genghis Khan was a man on a mission.

Clearly, Genghis could not have achieved this remarkable feat by adopting a soft and cuddly, let's hug-out our differences approach to his enemies, and by the time of his death it's estimated that the Great Khan's armies had ruthlessly killed an estimated 40 million people, about 11% of the world's population at the time. Negotiation techniques were not high on Genghis' list of key management skills.

However, although his methods may be a little difficult for today's environmentalists to accept, and are probably not the first option on their "Best ways to save the planet" manifesto, a recent study suggests that the Great Khan's slash and burn, mass slaughter approach to conquest likely removed over 700 million tons of carbon from the atmosphere as great swathes of cultivated land were wiped out and trees re-grew in their place. Genghis Khan may never have won the Nobel Peace prize, but he may well be a leading contender as the most effective eco-warrior of all time.

With the death of Genghis the position of Mongol Empire CEO fell in quick succession to a selection of his sons and grandsons, but after a civil war prompted by some Board-room sibling rivalry over succession, another of Genghis' many grandsons, Kublai Khan, eventually took over control the family business in 1264, and promptly continued to redraw maps of the world in favour of the Mongol Empire.

As a child Kublai had read some glossy travel brochures about Japan and heard good things about the local hotels and noodle shops, and so once settled into his new role, the new Mongol ruler turned his eyes on the land of the rising sun and wrote a nice letter to the then Emperor of Japan advising him of his intention to expand the Mongol Empire in his general direction. The note advised the Emperor that he should pay tribute to the Mighty Khan else he would be catching the next ferry over to complete a hostile take-over bid in person. Unfortunately, the Great Khan's emissaries returned from Japan without an answer, or indeed their heads.

At the time Kublai had his hands full unifying China under his rule, eventually founding the Yuan dynasty and adding to his growing list of titles that of Emperor of China, and so for the next six years he merely continued to send emissaries to Japan politely explaining his non-negotiable offshore plans. But the Japanese Emperor it seems would not allow them to even land in Japan and merely stamped his letters "return to sender".

By 1272 Kublai Khan was clearly running out of patience with Japan and decided to do what Mongol hoards do best when they don't get what they want, he started to plan for an invasion. However, given that there was a sizable stretch of water between him and Japan, Kublai needed to first build an Armada of war ships to transport his invasion force. By 1274 Kublai Khan had constructed an Armada of around 600 ships which he promptly filled with 40,000 men and horses, and pointed it in the general direction of Japan.

The invasion fleet quickly seized several of Japan's outlying Islands, and in true Mongol style slaughtered all the residents and burned down all the noodle shops before sailing on to Japan's main Islands, and on November 18, 1272, the Mongol Armada reached Hakata Bay, near the present-day city of Fukuoka on the island of Kyushu.

At Hakata Bay Kublai Khan and his Mongol army came face to face with Japan's Samurai warriors. The Samurai set out to fight the Mongol hoard according to their own code of Bushido, a warrior code of honour where a warrior would step out, announce his name and lineage, and prepare for one-on-one combat with a foe.

This bushido approach was all well and good when fighting other Samurai, but unfortunately for the Japanese the Mongols had not read that part of their Japanese guide book and so each time a lone samurai stepped forward to challenge them, the Mongols would first look at each other bemused, then simply attack him en-masse. The Samurai quickly drew back a few miles from the bay to have a quick rethink about the whole Bushido thing.

At this point the Samurai were probably no more than just a few days away from being forced to change their passports from Japanese to Mongol. They needed what's known in military circles as a miracle.

Then, just as the Japanese were quietly contemplating the likely effect of Mongol rule on local property prices, a driving wind and heavy rain began to lash the coast. Worried that the strong wind and high surf might drive their ships aground in Hakata Bay the Chinese and Korean sailors on board Kublai Khan's ships persuaded the Mongol generals to let them weigh anchor and head further out to sea to the safety of deeper water.

Unfortunately for Kublai Khan no one had bothered to check the long-range weather forecast, and what they thought was just a quick overnight storm was actually a full-blown typhoon. Kublai Khan's Armada promptly sailed head-long into the eye of the approaching typhoon, and two days later over half of his Armada and troops lay at the bottom of the Pacific. The battered Mongol survivors were forced to limp home red-faced, and Japan's noodle shops were spared the prospect of life under Mongol rule, at least for the time being.

Unfortunately for the Japanese, the Khan's had never been a family that took defeat very well, and on his return Kublai Khan promptly sent a six-man delegation to Japan demanding that the Japanese emperor personally travel to Kublai's capital in current day Beijing and kneel before him. The Japanese merely responded by beheading the Mongol diplomats and sending them back with a short "Thanks, but no thanks" note attached. If the telescope had been invented by then Kublai Khan could have used his to look out across the sea where he would have seen the entire Japanese imperial court collectively lifting up their Samurai skirts and mooning back at him.

This of course did little to improve Mongol-Japanese relations, and once the Great Khan had been calmed down enough to realize that killing everyone in the immediate 10 mile radius that vaguely looked Japanese was probably not such a great idea, he decided to establish a new government division, the aptly named, Ministry for Conquering Japan. The new ministry's job was simple, devise a plan to crush Japan once and for all.

Having taken themselves off on a blue-sky thinking away-day retreat, the collected members of the Ministry for Conquering Japan decided that their best chance of keeping their heads attached to their bodies was not to take any chances, and so devised a plan which called for an overwhelming two-pronged attack on Japan by not one, but two Mongol Armadas.

Thus, in the spring of 1281 the Mongol Empire sent two hastily prepared invasion forces bound for Japan, the first consisting of over 900 ships containing 40,000 Korean, Chinese, and Mongol troops set out from Korea, and the second with an even larger force of 100,000 troops which sailed from southern China in well over 3,500 ships. Confidence was high, and Kublai Khan was promised that he'd be in his new Japanese holiday home by the end of the summer.

The Korean fleet reached Hakata Bay on June 23, 1281, but the Armada from China was nowhere to be seen, and to make matters worse the Japanese had clearly been expecting the Mongol's invasion force, likely seen as a predictable consequence of sending back Kublai's diplomats minus their heads, and so were better prepared this time. A stalemate between the evenly-matched foes lasted for more than 50 days as the Korean fleet patiently waited for the expected Chinese reinforcements.

On the 12th August, 1281, the Mongols' main fleet finally landed to the west of Hakata Bay. Now faced with a force more than three times as large as their own, the Samurai were now in serious danger of being overrun and slaughtered. However, just when it appeared that Japan would very shortly be added to the growing Mongol map of the world, the top brass at the Ministry for Conquering Japan suddenly realized the one flaw in their "foolproof" plan. Once again, no one had bothered to check the weather forecast.

Three days later, on August 15, another typhoon roared ashore at Kyushu. Of the combined Armada's 4,400 ships only a few hundred managed to ride out the towering waves and vicious winds. Always better known for their horse-riding abilities than any aquatic skills, just about all the invading Mongol army also subsequently drowned in the storm, while the few thousand who made it to shore were hunted and killed without mercy by the Samurai. Very few ever returned to Mongol HQ back in China to tell the tale, and there were even fewer volunteers to be the one to tell Kublai Khan that his plans for a holiday home in Japan were now once again on hold.

For their part, the Japanese believed that their gods had now twice sent typhoons to save Japan from the Mongol hoards, calling the two storms kamikaze, or "divine winds". Kublai Khan meanwhile sensibly now disbanded his Ministry for Conquering Japan which by now had already seen all its top positions mysteriously become vacant, and understandably with few willing applicants for the now open positions anyway.

Raging Hormones Rule England For Thirty Years

Henry VIII sets new marriage record and changes the course of English history

When Henry VIII became King of England on 21st April 1509 he was only just 17 years old. He was witty, spoke several languages, wrote poetry, was a dab-hand at tennis and jousting, played the lute, and could throw some pretty mean shapes on the dance-floor. Henry was also considered something of a fine physical specimen for his day, he was tall, handsome, and in a time when men were admired more for the size of their calves than any six-pack or bulging biceps, Henry had calves like legs of ham. He was England's answer to the renaissance man, and he was now also a King, he was what your mom would call "quite the catch".

However, Henry had only become first in line to the throne on the death in 1502 of his elder brother, Arthur, whose death was officially reported as being due to the "sweating sickness" that was sweeping through Tudor England at the time. But given the fact that at the time he was a 15 year old boy with raging hormones and who had only just been married some 6 months earlier to a beautiful Spanish princess, Catherine of Aragon, with whom he had been honeymooning in Ludlow Castle ever since, many drew their own conclusions as to the likely cause of death.

Arthur had been betrothed to Catherine by his father, Henry VII, to help seal an alliance with Spain, and so keen to maintain the alliance the King now quickly moved to have his only other son, the future Henry VIII, marry his older brother's widow. Like all previous English Kings, Henry VII apparently liked to keep things in the family, and particularly so when the princess concerned had arrived with a very sizable dowry that would now have to be returned unless she stayed. In the King's eyes, the alliance, and of course the dowry, remained in place regardless of which future King of England she married. Thus, when he became King in 1509, Henry VIII married his brother's somewhat older "hand me down" widow. It would not be the last time Henry would walk down the aisle.

Apart from perfecting the "Royal wave" and cutting the ribbon at the opening of a few new schools and supermarkets, the only real role in Catherine's job description as a Tudor Queen of England was to supply her husband with a male son and heir. Catherine certainly didn't shy away from her duty, in the first 9 years of their marriage she conceived at least 6 times, but with only 1 child, a daughter, surviving beyond a few weeks, it was fast becoming clear to Henry that although Catherine was consistently receiving a 9/10 for effort at her year-end appraisals, she was failing miserably on any actual delivery.

In the meantime the handsome, virile, lute playing athlete Henry had been availing himself of the constant stream of pretty young maidens to be found at his court, and by 1527 his roving eye had settled on one of Catherine's ladies-in-waiting, Anne Boleyn. In many ways Anne was a strange choice for Henry's affections given that her looks were deemed plain at best, and she reportedly had six fingers on one hand and was thus considered by many to be a witch. However, Henry had already previously dipped his toe in the Boleyn gene pool with Anne's older sister, Mary, the fruits of which resulted in a bastard son, and so Henry likely sniffed a welcome family trait for popping out male offspring.

It was at this point that Henry's libido officially took over control and started running the country, and matters were made decidedly worse when Anne played her female Joker card and pronounced she would not let Henry have his kingly way with her until he made her his queen. Needing some quick inspiration Henry did what any red-blooded man would do under the circumstances, he turned to the Bible where he rather conveniently found a passage in Leviticus 20:21 which prohibited a man from marrying his brother's wife.

Henry quickly rattled off a letter to the Pope asking that he quickly annul his marriage to Catherine before God noticed what was happening in Henry's corner of God's kingdom and rained down a plague of locusts on Europe for his ungodly sin. To try and prevent Henry's attempt to divorce her on the grounds of "family used goods"

Catherine claimed that her marriage to Arthur had never been consummated and so was in effect not a marriage at all, but her claim was mostly just greeted with smirks and responses of "yeah, right".

Unfortunately the Pope decided that it would probably not be in his own best interests to be seen as the person responsible for making the King of Spain's Auntie Kath a middle-aged divorcee, and so for Henry the matter remained frustratingly unresolved. Eventually, Henry got fed up with having to take cold showers 3 times a day, and so in a bold move even for a lute playing King he declared himself the supreme Head of a new Church of England, which meant he no longer needed the permission of the Pope in Rome for anything, and especially over who he could, or could not, divorce.

The Pope was of course more than a little peeved by this and so duly excommunicated Henry from the Holy Roman Church, but it was of little consequence to Henry, he was now supreme head of his own shiny new church, and whose first order of business was to declare his marriage to Catherine null and void. And so in January 1533 Henry set off down the aisle for the second time, this time to marry Anne Boleyn. Catherine was banished from court and spent the rest of her days wandering around a succession of remote, cold, and damp castles wondering just where it all went wrong.

With the sudden joint release of several years of pent up frustration, Anne was quickly pregnant, but disappointingly for Henry the result was yet another daughter, Elizabeth. Two further pregnancies only ended in miscarriage and when Henry discovered the second baby had been a boy, he became convinced that the marriage was cursed, and that maybe Anne had a broomstick and wand hidden away in her wardrobe after all. Unfortunately for Anne, she was proving no more able to provide Henry with a male heir than wife No. 1 had.

Henry was still desperate for a male heir, and blaming Anne for the lack of male offspring he turned his attentions to Anne's lady-in-waiting Jane Seymour and started to look for a way to end his marriage to the wicked Witch of Hampton Court. This time however he wasn't going to mess around with any time consuming divorce proceedings, and Anne was promptly arrested on some quickly manufactured charges of adultery. Not wanting to take any chances with the case being thrown out of court, Henry played it safe and ensured that a total of 5 men were named as Anne's adulterous lovers and tagged her own brother onto the list just for good measure. Anne was duly convicted and imprisoned in the Tower of London, and on the 19th May 1536 was separated from her head.

Henry's marriage to Anne had lasted less than the time it took him to actually free himself enough to marry her, a process that saw him break with the Roman Catholic church and unwittingly set England down the path of the Reformation. If it wasn't for Anne Boleyn all England would likely still be Roman Catholic, everyone would be eating fish on Friday's, would all come from families with at least 12 siblings, and would all probably be driving around with a bobble-head of the Pope on the dashboard of their car.

Within 24 hours of Anne Boleyn's execution, Jane Seymour and Henry were formally betrothed, and a short 10 days later finding that the Vegas 24-hour "Quickie" Wedding Chapel was still unfortunately under construction, Henry and Jane instead chose to sprint down the aisle at Whitehall in London.

In October 1537, Henry's prayers were answered and a prince was born and later christened Edward. Unfortunately, Henry never got to play happy families with Jane and Edward, Jane Seymour was to die just 12 days later. If it wasn't one thing it was another.

Henry blubbered for weeks mourning Jane Seymour's death, which unfortunately all became a bit embarrassing around court with Henry suddenly bursting into tears during meetings with foreign ambassadors, or found still in his pyjamas and hugging his pillow late into the afternoon. Eventually Thomas Cromwell, Henry's right hand man, could stand it no more and advised Henry that the best way to get over Jane was to get back in the saddle as quickly as possible.

To this end Cromwell proposed that Henry kill two birds with one stone and attempt to establish ties with the German Protestant alliance against Catholic Rome by marrying the German princess Anne of Cleves. Henry put down his pillow just long enough to agree but only on the condition that he first see a portrait of the proposed princess.

A portrait was duly commissioned to be painted by the famed portrait artist of the day Hans Holbein. The portrait showed Anne of Cleves to be a vision of beauty, Henry quickly stopped blubbering for Jane Seymour and set about planning for his wedding night, while Thomas Cromwell rubbed his hands together over another little piece of business well done. Then Anne of Cleves arrived at court.

It seemed that on seeing Anne in the flesh Henry quickly noticed that Holbein had not quite captured that special "looks a bit like a horse" quality that he now saw standing before him. Henry was less than pleased, the marriage was a disaster and Henry divorced Anne a few months later. Henry blamed Cromwell for the mismatch and so naturally had him executed for treason.

Having drawn a complete blank with the "Flanders Mare", Henry decided to look for a somewhat younger model, and his attentions turned to Catherine Howard, an 18 year old lady-in-waiting to the now homeward bound Anne of Cleves. Catherine was young and beautiful but rumour had it that she had already been around the block a few times with the young bucks at court, but regardless, Henry set his heart of Catherine, and what the King wants the King generally gets, and 16 days after he waved goodbye to Anne of Cleves as she got into her horse-box back to Germany, Henry married Catherine Howard. He was 49 and she was 18, what could possibly go wrong?

From the outset it was clear this was never going to be a good match. While Catherine was in her prime the once swim-suit model Henry was now a middle-aged super-sized Henry and was clearly not quite the catch he was 20 years before. Henry's once 32 inch waist was now fast approaching Zeppelin-like proportions, and those calves that used to make Tudor women swoon were now covered in rather less attractive open-sores. He was now a grumpy, short-tempered binge eater whose weight had ballooned to the point where he now had to be winched onto his horse. Most at court could see that the marriage was not going to end well, and likely with Catherine's head separated from her young body. True to the bookie's odds, Catherine was executed for adultery and treason on February 13th, 1542, their marriage had lasted less than 18 months.

Probably now realizing that neither his health or his age were up to such younger models, Henry looked for a somewhat more girl-next-door, sisterly-type for his next bride. Catherine Par was a twice widowed, childless 31 year old who was employed in the household of Mary, Henry's daughter by Catherine of Aragon. She was smart, matronly, and managed not to feint in horror every time she was in the presence of the now very over weight, bad smelling, ulcer-ridden, belligerent King. She was ideal. They were married 12th July 1543, although it's unlikely that Henry stood to take his vows.

At this point you could now count the number of Henry's marriages on the right hand of his second wife. Catherine however was destined to be Henry's last, she nursed him through his final years and outlived him by a year. Henry died on 28 January 1547 and was succeeded by his son, Edward VI, the only son he had managed to conjure up from a total of 6 marriages.

Henry VIII began his reign as a handsome young king beloved by his people, and ended it as a grotesquely fat tyrant who was feared by all who knew him, and with five failed marriages behind him. Marriages often do fail, however, Henry VIII's abject failure to hang on to a spouse for any length of time surpassed all expectations particularly in terms of the impact each failed marriage would have, as where in general the damage is usually limited to bitter arguments over who gets the CD's, the car, and the kids, in Henry's case the fallout was to shape a whole nation.

Exploring Can Be A Dangerous Business

Great Expeditions that ended in heroic failure

Being an explorer can be a risky business. By definition your place of work is in areas where no one else has ever dared to venture before, usually it's completely inhospitable, painfully difficult to get to, is off the chart of any known map or Satellite-Navigation system, and quite frankly offers no guarantee that if by some miracle you do arrive safely at your destination you won't be met by a tribe of hungry cannibals craving some exotic Johnny-Foreigner meat.

Even if you do manage to safely negotiate whatever jungles, swamps, ice-packs, mountains, man-eating wildlife, or diseases that stand between you and your unexplored, uncharted destination allowing you to plant your "I was here first" flag in the ground, unless you also safely get home again to tell the tale it all would have been a bit of a waste of time anyway.

Quite frankly, if you in anyway like Michael Buble, folk music, or salad, maybe enjoy a quiet evening of poetry reading, are scared of spiders or heights, or have an unhealthy attachment to the contents of your fridge, then I would suggest that a career as an Explorer is probably not for you. You'd be better off to just sit comfortably in a warm office and wait for the airlines and tour operators to safely add that particular area of interest to their list of all-inclusive 5-star package-holiday destinations.

In fact, should your plans in any way include getting back home again safely, as an explorer you're faced with only two possibly outcomes. Firstly you achieve your goal, get home safely, and are hailed a hero. Or, you fail to reach your goal, and are forced to return home under the cover of darkness with your head bowed low and be subsequently made to wear a sign around your neck for the rest of your life advertising your abject failure.

Perhaps this is why most explorers meticulously plan their outward journey, but pay little attention to the logistics of the return leg. Because regardless of whether they successfully get to plant their flag or not, if they fail to make it back home alive they know they will likely be hailed as a hero anyway. History is littered with explorers who woefully failed in their primary objective, yet still managed to attain hero-like status back at home purely based on the fact that despite their failure they still manfully fought against all the odds, right up to the point where they were eaten by cannibals, fell off the mountain, succumbed to unbearable disease, starvation or injury, or heroically sacrificed themselves in the hope that others may still succeed.

Take for instance the British climbers George Mallory and Andrew Irvine who attempted to become the first outside of goats and yaks to climb Mt. Everest. They set off on 8th June 1924 with a couple of oxygen bottles, a few thread-bare ropes, and a second-hand ice- pick, wearing only some sturdy hiking boots, some corduroy slacks, and a couple of pairs of woolly sweaters their mums had knitted for them. They were last seen alive at 12:50pm seemingly within spitting distance of the summit, but then clouds rolled in and they were never seen again.

Both were hailed as heroes back in England with numerous memorials subsequently being named after them, including Mt. Mallory and Mt. Irvine in the Sierra Nevada, California. We will never know if they actually made it to the summit, but of course that merely added to the mystique, and regardless of whether they met their deaths on the way up or on the way down from the peak, from that point on they were ensured an iconic place in mountaineering history.

Nobody cared whether they were nothing more than a couple of ill-equipped, ill-prepared, British ramblers who found themselves 26,000 feet higher off the ground than common sense and their equipment dictated they really should have been. They died doing plucky heroic things with nothing more than equipment they found in their garden shed and a stiff upper lip, and that was enough to make them heroes in everyone's book.

Probably the greatest of all heroic failures was that of Sir Robert Falcon Scott's 1910-12 Antarctic expedition to try and be the first to reach the South Pole. Scott and his team did actually reach the South pole on 17th January, 1912, only to find that a rival Norwegian party led by Roald Amundsen had beaten them there by 33 days, and who was by then already safely at home warming his toes by the fire, and giving glowing interviews to the press.

Understandably not in the mood for a party, Scott left the champagne on ice, mumbled something distinctly anti-Norwegian, and then turned his ill-equipped and malnourished team of plucky Brits around to start the long 1,500 km journey back to home-base.

Conditions on the return journey were particularly severe. Every night the plucky explorers would climb into their flimsy tents and take off their socks to find that yet another toe had come off due to frostbite. By March, one of the party, Laurence Oates was suffering from severe frostbite and knew he was holding back his companions. He bravely told the others that he was just going off for a little stroll and "may be some time", and then walked off into the freezing conditions never to be seen again. The remaining three men, including Scott, died of starvation and exposure in their tent a few days later on 29 March 1912.

Amundsen's victory and Scott's defeat have acquired mythical status over the years, a battle between cold, Scandinavian efficiency and cheery British amateur have-a-go pluck.

Despite the embarrassment of arriving at the South pole only to find a Norwegian flag already there to greet them, back in England Scott and his team were hailed as heroes, sacrificing themselves in the pursuit of British glory. But where Scott's party failed in its primary objective and perished on the ice, Amundsen's team not only reached the pole first, it also handled the expedition with greater ease and also emerged from the expedition without the loss of a single human life or toe.

Any betting man with even the slightest idea about ice, cold, and attempting to travel long distances under the worst of both, would have put their mortgage on Scott's heroic but ultimately 3rd-rate, ill-conceived expedition coming in a distant second to the single-minded ruthless efficiency of Amundsen's party.

Scott's expedition was likely doomed from the outset. He had inexplicably chosen pony's to pull his supplies rather than the usual Antarctic friendly husky dogs, he insisted on collecting rocks along the way for later scientific examination, and expected his team of to merrily ski most of the way to the pole.

Unfortunately, the pony's proved next to useless on ice and snow and quickly died of exhaustion, reducing the party to man-hauling all the supplies and equipment themselves unaided. The collected rocks only added more weight to the loads and slowed them down even more, it seems that only one of his party could properly navigate their way out of a paper bag, and to make matters worse Scott quickly discovered that most of his men had never even seen a pair of skis before let alone actually be able to use them.

It was amazing that they even found the pole at all, but it came as no surprise that the ill-fated but plucky explorers became instant heroes, and were elevated to God-like status once their frozen fate was finally discovered the following year.

Even explorers whose ambitions clearly out-weighed what common-sense they had resulting in a fairly predictable one-way voyage of exploration, are elevated to hero status purely based on their blatant disregard for their own safety in pursuit of their goal.

One such example is the Swedish explorer Salomon August Andrée, who in July 1897 set off to be the first man to reach the North pole. Andrée was a middle-aged Swedish engineer captivated by the promise and possibilities of technology, and who came up with a radical idea. Why not give all that long trudge in the snow carrying food and supplies a miss and simply fly in a hydrogen balloon to become the first to discover the North Pole?

For years explorers had attempted to reach the Pole over-land, and all had either quickly turned back to await the invention of better technology and warmer clothes, or ended up as ice-statues. Andrée reasoned that an air expedition would eliminate much of the risk associated with travelling across a frozen ice-pack for months on end dragging your equipment and cornflakes with you.

And so, on a windy day in July 1897 Andrée and two like-minded colleagues climbed into the basket of a 67-foot-diameter balloon on Danes Island in the Svalbard archipelago north of Sweden. The team packed wooden sledges, food for several months, carrier pigeons to relay messages, and even a tuxedo Andrée hoped to wear at the pole to celebrate the success of the expedition. As journalists and well-wishers cheered and waved goodbye, they soared into the air, fully expecting to gently float to the North Pole, take a few nice photos, and then gently float back again.

Unfortunately Andrée had not considered the effect of local weather conditions, freezing fog and ice, and the fact that balloons are steered by the prevailing winds and not those hanging on for dear life in the basket below. Within 3 days the balloon was blown hopelessly off course and skimmed the ground under the added weight of the accumulated ice. Eventually the expedition was forced to land on the Arctic pack when their 67 foot balloon eventually gave up and became a 67 foot rug.

To Andrée's credit, plans had been made for such an eventuality with such items as guns, skis, snowshoes, a tent, and 4-months of provisions, packed for the trip. So now the 3 intrepid explorers were forced to give up their lofty goal and trek south in search of civilization and safety.

Unfortunately, after several weeks of marching south they realized that the pack-ice they were walking on was moving in the opposite direction to the way they wanted to go. Not ideal, and so their progress south had been minimal. They changed direction and finally spotted a remote island, White Island, in early October. However, the arctic winter was rapidly approaching and far better shelter and clothing was needed than a tent and a tuxedo if they were to survive. Nothing further was heard of the expedition for the next 33 years.

In 1930 sealers stumbled across the frozen corpses of Andrée and his crew, along with their cameras and diaries, which revealed that they'd been forced to land on pack ice a full 298 miles shy of the North Pole and had eventually succumbed to the Arctic winter.

However, despite the abject failure of their expedition, the eventual homecoming of the bodies of Andrée and his colleagues was a grand national event. King Gustaf V of Sweden delivered an oration, and the explorers received a funeral held with great honours. The fact that the whole plan was ill-conceived and doomed to failure from the minute Andrée had first uttered the phrase, "I've have an idea", was conveniently overlooked.

Overall, explorers do not have a great track record. In reality only one explorer can be the first to discover, climb, or reach, anywhere or anything. The rest are doomed to second place at best, and if they are lucky being remembered for their heroic endeavours, but which unfortunately usually means they never actually made it back.

A life of exploring is clearly a dangerous calling, with little reward except for the lucky few, and with a life expectancy pretty much on a par with a Russian Cosmonaut or a Mexican Cartel drug dealer. So, after much careful thought in the bath this morning, I have concluded that a life of adventure and exploration is not one I shall be considering anytime soon, and for the time being I will just be sticking to my National Geographic magazines and the Indiana Jones trilogy.

Scotland's Failed Empire

The Scottish Darién Scheme

Scotland at the end of the 17th Century was quite frankly in a bit of a mess. The big boys of Europe were all busy reaping the rewards of the New World, the Indies, and Africa, happily trading, slaving, and exploiting native populations, and generally getting fat off their ever growing empires. But Scotland was fast becoming Europe's poor relative with decades of warfare, years of famine, trade crippled by European in-fighting, and arguments amongst the clans about whether underpants should be allowed to be worn under kilts, all of which had left Scotland weak, poor, still somewhat chilly around the nether-regions, and effectively the lame duck of Europe.

Frankly, if Scotland had been a horse it would have been put down. Clearly something had to be done, some way had to be found to revive Scotland's economic fortunes before it got swallowed up by its much richer southern neighbour and renamed as "Scotshire".

The first bright spark to come up with an idea was a financial adventurer called William Paterson, a Scot who had made his name south of the border working for the "old-enemy" as one of the founding directors of the Bank of England. However, Paterson's passed indiscretions were quickly forgiven when he returned to Edinburgh in 1695 with an audacious scheme that promised to see Scotland transformed from being Europe's Council Estate into Europe's major trade broker.

In reality Paterson was nothing more than a 17th century second-hand car salesman, and his great scheme to turn Scotland into a European super-power was ill thought out and naive, and as it turned out, ultimately doomed from the start. But Scotland needed a miracle, and given that the only other alternative on the table seemed to revolve around trying to convince the world that the new must-have fashion item was a kilt, Paterson's plan looked to be the best option.

Whilst in London, Paterson had met a sailor who had spun him a yarn about a sun-drenched paradise on the Isthmus of Panama, with a sheltered bay, friendly locals, fertile land, where the sun shone every day, and with long sandy beaches with not a German beach towel insight. This little piece of heaven was called Darién, and Paterson's eyes immediately lit up with dollar signs believing he had found the ideal spot for a Pacific Trading colony, and the answer to Scotland's dreams.

As an ex-city wide-boy Paterson knew that trade with the incredibly lucrative Pacific markets was currently a hugely expensive business for Europe's big boys. All European merchant ships trading with the Pacific currently had to first make a lengthy and hazardous trip round the Cape Horn on the southern tip of South America to reach the Pacific ocean, adding months, and cost, to the journey.

If Paterson could establish a colony at Darién on Panama's Atlantic coast, on the thin strip of land that separated the Pacific and Atlantic oceans by a mere 30 miles, an overland route connecting the two oceans could be created, greatly speeding up the Pacific trade route. All Scotland had to do was to stick a flag in the ground at Darién, setup a toll-booth, and then sit back and watch the money roll in. The plan seemed fool-proof, it would give Scotland control of Pacific trade routes, move it from Europe's 2nd division straight to the top of the Premiership overnight, while at the same time lining the pockets of all involved, and in particular those of Mr. Paterson himself.

The idea naturally proved hugely popular, and there was a great rush to invest in the new Company of Scotland, the company founded in June 1695 to fund and manage the scheme. But Paterson had neglected to tell anyone that the Spanish had actually already laid claim to Panama, and that actually he also knew nothing about Darién itself other than what a drunken sailor had told him over a few whiskeys and a haggis in the pub. Such minor details were soon to prove a bit of an issue.

And it was not just the Spanish who were about to react rather unfavourably to Scotland's grand scheme. The English East India Company, fearing the loss of its monopoly on British trade to the Indies were also not best pleased about their kilt-wearing neighbour's scheme, and successfully lobbied the English Parliament, which flexed its parliamentary muscles and forced many of the schemes English and foreign investors to withdraw.

Undaunted, Paterson and his colleagues turned to the Scottish people for financial support. The Scots as a race have always been known for their financial prudence, but clearly having short arms and deep pockets does not seemingly cure gullibility, and the Scottish people, both rich and poor, tripped over their kilts to jump on the Darién bandwagon in what they saw as Scotland's great opportunity to establish itself on the world stage. Within six months £400,000 had been raised, which amounted to approximately a fifth of all the wealth in Scotland at the time. The collective savings of most of the Scottish nation were now riding on Paterson's scheme.

By 1698, five ships had been hastily built and packed with 1,200 willing volunteers, and set sail for the coast of Panama with the dream of Scotland's future empire resting on their shoulders. The ships made landfall off the coast of Darién on November 2, 1698. The settlers christened their new home "New Caledonia" , and quickly got down to the business of making Scotland a world super-power.

Then the glory of bad planning and even worse leadership raised its ugly head and went to work. First, they constructed a fort in an area with no fresh water supply. Then they tried to set up fields to grow maize and yams, which they quickly discovered none of them actually knew how to do. They tried to trade with the local Indians, who just laughed at the kilts, sporrans, and the "I love Scotland" tee-shirts they had brought with them to trade, while the long sandy beaches and fertile land in reality proved to be more mosquito infested mangroves and bogs. It was not a great start.

Then the spring 1699 brought torrential rain, and with it disease. By March 1699, more than 200 colonists had already died, mostly from disease and the fact that the settlers clearly had no idea how to store food in the heat and humidity of Panama, and so most of it would spoil, making the hunger situation much worse.

To make matters even worse, the ships sent out to trade for supplies returned with news that all English ships and colonies had been forbidden to trade with the settlement by order of the King who didn't want to upset Spain. One ship didn't even bother to return at all.

The final straw came when the colonists received news that the Spanish were planning an attack on the colony. On hearing the news, the settlers did the only sensible thing they could do and took to the sea in panic, abandoning the settlement after only 8 months. Of the four ships that fled the colony only 1 ship actually made it safely back to Scotland, with less than 300 souls on board.

Once home those that returned were not greeted warmly by Scotland. Most of the Scottish population had invested their life savings in the Darién Scheme, and they did not take kindly to the settlers abandoning Scotland's one shot at becoming a world player in less than eight months, regardless of their stories of disease, starvation, inhospitable land, and locals who didn't have either the expected movie-star looks or same fondness for kilts. Those that had returned were considered a disgrace to their country, with many of them being disowned by their families, and were summarily forced to listen to bagpipe music 24 hours a day as punishment.

To make matters worse, word of the failed colony did not get back to Scotland in time to prevent a second wave of 1,000 settlers shipping out, and who thus arrived in Darién to a decrepit ghost town that they now had to rebuild. But the same problems persisted, and after an attack by the Spanish in January of 1700, they too took to their ships and abandoned the colony for good, taking with them only what they could carry and sailing back to Scotland as quickly as their ships could take them. Once again, only a few hundred had survived.

In reality, the men and women sent out to Darién were completely unprepared for the harshness of the territory in which they found themselves, and the collapse in discipline, starvation, and rampant disease which afflicted them were just the natural consequence of throwing people brought up in a cold, Scottish highland climate, on a constant diet of porridge and haggis, into a tropical nightmare full of new diseases, mosquitoes, with only mangoes and fish to eat, and with no manual or Bear Grylls on hand to help them. It would be a bit like sending Prince Charles to go live on the dole in an inner-city slum without his army of servants, cooks, and valets, except that he would probably last considerably less than 8 months.

On top of this, the tiny outpost population faced the constant threat of attack from the Spanish, and received absolutely no support from the English colonies which had been ordered to wave politely, but not to aid them in any way, shape, or form. Ultimately, the Darién venture was a complete disaster for Scotland. The last time someone got it all this wrong his name was Neville Chamberlin and he was waving a piece of paper in the air. The whole plan was effectively doomed from the day they set sail from Scotland.

The blow to Scottish morale and coffers was incalculable. The company had lost over £250,000, primarily made up of the life savings of the Scottish people, and its failure left the entire nation almost completely ruined. Scotland would not feel such shame again until 1996 when England knocked them out of the European Soccer Championships.

Effectively bankrupt, Scotland was now left completely incapable of surviving as a nation in its own right. Eventually, to stop the increasingly rude letters from their local Bank manager, Scotland was forced to go sporran in hand to their fat-cat neighbours south of the border looking for a hand out. England agreed to bail out the destitute Scots, but would do so only if Scotland conceded to the Act of Union, an Act of Parliament which joined Scotland with England in a single united kingdom which was to be called "Great Britain". Scotland cleared its debts, but was now forever more doomed to be the junior partner in the mighty union of Great Britain.

In an ironic twist, just over 200 years later the French and Americans combined to build the Panama Canal, a 48 mile ship canal across the middle of Panama that connects the Atlantic to the Pacific Ocean, and which remains a key conduit for international maritime trade even today. The Panama Canal was officially opened to great fanfare on August 15, 1914, Scotland did not attend. To this day, the land where the Darién colony was built remains virtually uninhabited by anything other than snakes and mosquitoes.

Into The Valley Of Death Rode The Six Hundred

The Charge of the Light Brigade

By the late 1800's the once mighty Turkish Ottoman Empire was in decline. At its height during the 16th century under the control of the modestly named Suleiman the Magnificent the Ottoman Empire had ruled over the Middle East, North Africa, Turkey, Greece, and the Balkans, while quietly keeping a controlling influence over every Turkish and Greek kebab shop from London to Moscow.

However, due to a run of Sultans that proved to fall somewhat short of "Magnificent", the Empire was now in decline, and in July 1853, sniffing an opportunity for a quick Balkan land-grab the Russian Tsar, Nicholas I, ordered his army to march into Ottoman held Moldavia cut down the Ottoman flag and hoist his own. Turkey was understandably miffed, promptly declared war on Russia, but then helplessly watched as the Russians promptly sent the Ottoman fleet to the bottom of the Black Sea.

Alarmed at the thought of the Russians snapping up all the best holiday homes around the Black sea, and discovering that a key strategic partner along their key Trade routes to India and the East was now suddenly down one navy, both Britain and France sent a strongly worded letter to Russia advising them that they much preferred things to stay the way they were and to kindly stop all plans to hoist Russian flags all over the Balkans.

Unfortunately, all the Russian top-brass were away looking at Real-estate opportunities around the Black sea coast, and so having received an out-of-office response from Russian Military HQ the British and French quickly moved to Plan B. In March 1854, they joined forces with Turkey and declared war on Russia, fully expecting that with their naval supremacy they would destroy the Russian naval power in the Black sea and so secure a quick victory.

Strangely, Britain and France now found themselves on the same side of an armed conflict for the first time since they both tried to hold off the might of the Roman Empire under Julius Caesar almost 2,000 years earlier. Things had not gone that well all those years ago for that particular Celtic-Gaul alliance, and it didn't take long for things to start to go wrong this time either.

The allied forces of Britain, France, and Turkey were mustered at Varna in Bulgaria and prepared for an all-out assault on Russian forces in the Crimea to seize the Russian naval base at Sevastopol. However, on arrival it quickly became apparent that the French had forgotten to bring their cavalry, the British did bring their cavalry but forgot to pack any winter clothes or bunks for them to sleep in, and the Turks forgot to bring any food. Everyone it seems forgot to bring any medical supplies.

Allied leaders fired off some accusatory glances across the table at each other as they passed around the port and cigars, but the whole administrative shambles was summed up when the British sent some shiny new boots for its troops on the ground but managed to only ship 5,000 right boots, the matching left boots apparently remaining in stores back in London apparently awaiting appropriate paperwork.

Fortunately, the Russians proved even more incompetent and disorganized than the allies, and the whole Crimean war would have just been laughed off as one big embarrassing disaster on both sides were it not for the fact that due to such incompetence over 25,000 British, 100,000 French, and up to a million Russian soldiers died during the ensuing conflict, and almost all to disease, neglect, and ill-treatment.

At one point more soldiers were dying from the medical treatment they were (or were not) receiving in the field hospitals than on the battlefield itself, and the British government were finally forced to send out Florence Nightingale, a campaigner for better nursing, who's wandering up and down the medical wards at night with a lamp seemed to help.

By 14th September 1854 the allies had finally managed to pull together a joint invasion force and landed north of Sevastopol, with the British troops in their mismatched boots establishing an operating base at Balaklava and the French minus their cavalry at Kamiesch

Bay, all ready to lay siege to Sevastopol, quickly defeat the Ruskies, and be home in time for Christmas.

However, on the 25th October the Russian army unexpectedly moved towards the British lines at Balaklava, and the ensuing battle was to become the scene of one of the British Army's most notorious and embarrassing engagements. Although on the plus side the cold weather and lack of winter clothing did force British troops to cut eye-holes in their woollen socks and put them over their heads to keep warm, thus gifting the fashion world the woollen multi-purpose head-gear we now know as the Balaklava.

Battle lines at the Battle of Balaklava were drawn with the main British and Turkish forces, including the cavalry led by Earl Lucan, at one end of the valley, with the Russians at the other end, with both armies having heavily-armed, well defended, strategic positions on the valley ridges. Early in the battle a small Russian force attacked one such strategic position manned by Turks who promptly demonstrated one of the main reasons why the Ottoman Empire was on the decline and fled. The Russians then gratefully started to make off with the guns, cannon, and ammunition which the Turks had so conveniently left behind in their haste to be somewhere else.

Sat high on the ridge above the British position was the now rather elderly Lord Raglan, the Supreme Commander of the British forces in the Crimea, who was a veteran of Waterloo and who found it hard to forget that the French were now fighting on the same side and so kept referring to them as "the enemy". Raglan saw the Russians making off with their military booty, mumbled something about Turks and backbone, and then ordered that the Russians be quickly engaged to prevent the loss of guns.

Unfortunately the order Raglan gave was at best vague and was hastily scribbled by General Airey, Raglan's Quartermaster General, who only confused the order even more. The order read;

'Lord Raglan wishes the cavalry to advance rapidly to the front - follow the enemy and try to prevent the enemy carrying away the guns. Troop Horse artillery may accompany. French cavalry is on your left. Immediate!'

Captain Nolan, aide-de-camp to General Airey, took the order to Earl Lucan who had been patiently twiddling his thumbs down in the valley waiting for something for his cavalry to do other than sit and admire their new right boots. Lucan read the order, passed it to Lord Cardigan the Commander of the Light Cavalry Brigade, who also read it, and then the two of them stared at each other with the bemused look of a goldfish.

Rather crucially, the order did not say which guns to advance on, or indeed even where they were. Although Raglan from his vantage point could clearly see the Russians scampering off with their Turkish booty, Cardigan and Lucan camped down in the valley could not see them, the only guns they could see were the heavy artillery of the full Russian army two miles away at the other end of the valley.

When Lucan asked what guns the order referred to, Nolan rather unhelpfully just vaguely waved his arm in the general direction of the valley and said "There!". Cardigan and Lucan assumed, therefore, that they were being ordered to take the guns at the end of the valley, the main Russian force.

As a rule, cavalrymen generally do not fare well when faced with heavy artillery, which is why basic military tactics, and actually just plain common sense, dictate that cavalry should not attack such a force, particularly at the end of a valley where the enemy also has strategic gun emplacements setup all along the length of the valley ridges. It looked like exactly what it was, a suicide mission, still, as British military tradition dictated Lucan believed that the orders, regardless of how foolish they appeared to be, were to be obeyed.

Lucan ordered Cardigan to lead his Light Horse Brigade, comprising of 673 men, down the valley at a canter and to attack the heavy artillery two miles away at the other end of the valley. Rather than question the sanity of the order, Cardigan accepted his fate, ordered his horse saddled, and quickly ran back to his tent to change his underwear before relaying the order to his men.

Cardigan led the charge up the length of the valley and between the two rows of Russian artillery on the valley's ridges, being joined at the front by Nolan who now suddenly realising that the charge was aimed at the wrong target and heading towards certain death was last seen rushing across in front of Cardigan in a vain attempt to stop the charge. Unfortunately Nolan was almost immediately killed by an artillery shell and the cavalry continued on its course.

At first, the Russians could not believe their eyes and presumed the British Cavalrymen must have been drunk, and so did not all fire at once. But then seeing that the Light Brigade were not just out on a drunken dare, and were actually intent on attacking the main Russian artillery, the massacre began. The Light Brigade were bombarded from all sides and not surprisingly suffered heavy casualties.

Lucan, who had conveniently stayed behind rather than lead the charge himself, failed to provide any support for Cardigan. The fact that Cardigan and Lucan were actually brothers-in-law who disliked each other intensely ever since Cardigan had separated from Lucan's youngest sister, clearly played no role in Lucan's decision.

Miraculously, the Light Brigade did actually reach the main Russian artillery battery and even managed to scatter some of the gunners, but the badly mauled brigade was forced to retreat almost immediately. The whole event was a pointless fiasco, a bit like cutting off your hands to save money on gloves, and only a charge by French cavalry saved the Light Brigade from total destruction.

The brigade was not completely destroyed, but did suffer terribly, with 118 men killed, 127 wounded and about 60 taken prisoner. After regrouping, only 195 men were still with horses. The futility of the action and its reckless bravery allegedly prompted the on-looking French Marshal Pierre Bosquet, to state "It is magnificent, but it is not war, it is madness".

Unfortunately for the bungling British military top-brass such disasters were now not going unreported back in Britain. Not only was the Crimean war photographed, but the advent of the telegraph now meant that the press could send back regular reports to Britain where the all too regular reports of administrative bungling, mistreatment of the lower ranks, and the stubborn adherence to rather stupid orders, had many a Victorian choking on their breakfast marmalade.

Of course the other problem with such uncensored reports in the press was that they were also then readily available to the enemy who now could find details of all British and French troop movements on the front pages of the British daily papers. It appears to have been not too arduous a task to be a Russian spy during the Crimean war, requiring merely loose change enough each day to go and buy the daily newspaper.

The Crimean War eventually ended in the spring of 1856 with the Russians defeated and an agreement that the Black sea was to remain neutral. The Russians did get to keep their holiday homes but agreed to only fly the Russian flag during holidays or the World Cup. However, wrangling over the details of the ill-fated "Charge of the Light Brigade" and who was at fault continued into the following decade.

In reality all involved needed to share some responsibility. Raglan's order was imprecise, Airey's drafting of the order was ambiguous, Nolan failed to explain the order to Lucan adequately, Lucan failed to question Nolan properly to establish his commander's intent, and Cardigan failed to seek adequate clarification from Lucan who had also failed to provide support from the horse artillery as mentioned in the order. However, on the assumption that he wasn't around anymore to cause a fuss, having rather conveniently been killed in the ill-fated charge, the official military conclusion was that it was all Nolan's fault. For his part Raglan insisted it was the French.

Paintings, poems, and movies of the day's events followed, all of which chose to depict the 600 cavalrymen charging the full might of the Russian army as heroic figures, wildly outnumbered yet continuing to display unquestioning loyalty to Queen and country. In short they focused almost entirely on the heroic rather than the idiotic side of the whole debacle.

Only in Britain could one of the most embarrassing military incidents of all time be held up as a shining example of honour, heroism, and an often quoted source of national pride. Political spin-doctors still tip their hats in respect even today.

The English Beat France With Only Two Fingers

The Battle of Agincourt

The Hundred Year's War was actually a whole series of conflicts waged on and off from 1337 to 1453 between almost five generations of English and French kings, primarily over whose was the rightful royal-bottom to be sitting on the French throne.

If nothing else, the war proved at least 2 things. Firstly, that both France or England were clearly as stubborn as a couple of coked-up mules, and secondly that the people in charge at the "Ministry for Naming Wars" could not do basic arithmetic. The endless battles over 116 years meant that for decades the momentum swung back and forth between the two sides like a mediaeval game of high-stakes ping-pong, until in 1413 England crowned a new King who had a rather silly pudding-bowl haircut but who proved rather good at winning battles, and who would turn the tide of the erroneously titled war very much in England's favour.

In a time when success as an English King was still very much measured by how many battles you had fought and won, Henry V was a true hero, particularly when victories against France counted as double. Henry V was England's ultimate warrior King, courageous, inspirational, and a master tactician, in any list of England's greatest heroes he would be right up there with Boudicca, Winston Churchill, Julie Andrews, and David Beckham.

By 1415, Henry V had decided it was time once more to kick the Hundred Years war back into high gear in pursuit of his rather tenuous claim to the French throne. At the time France was in political turmoil with internal disputes, and the current King of France, Charles VI, was a half mad idiot who had lost all control of his court, so it seemed as a good a time as any to quickly sail over to France to kill a few Frenchies, bring back the French crown, a few bottles of duty-free wine, and a big lump of cheese for the wife. It was during this campaign that Henry V had his greatest away win, at the Battle of Agincourt.

But Henry's victory at Agincourt owed as much to French ineptitude as it did to his ability to give rousing speeches, and the battle became a turning point not only in the Hundred Years war, but also in the way battles would be fought going forward.

In fact the whole campaign did not start that well for Henry. The first engagement with the French was at Harfleur where Henry laid siege to the town and starved the local residents into submission. Unfortunately the lengthy siege also resulted in many of his own soldiers being left weakened by dysentery and illness and having to be sent back home to their mums. What was left of Henry's army, although victorious, was now weakened and somewhat lighter in number.

Despite having secured Harfleur, Henry now realized that the full might of the French army was now heading his way, and numbered at least five times the size of his remaining force who were by now nearly all suffering from dysentery and so spending more time on the toilet than on the field practising how to fight the French.

Henry didn't need to be a master tactician to realize that he was now facing an imminent massacre, and so he planned a hasty retreat to Calais where his waiting ships could get him and the remainder of his army safely back to England and some decent toilet facilities. Unfortunately for Henry, the French forces intercepted his army en route, and on 25th October, 1415, he was forced to stand and fight at a little backwater of Northern France called Agincourt.

Henry's army was vastly outnumbered, they were tired from the forced march from Harfleur in the rush to try and catch the early ferry back to England, and most were now suffering from dysentery and so were more concerned about the location of the nearest toilets rather than any French soldiers. Yet despite such a seemingly advantageous position, the French still somehow managed to grasp defeat out of the jaws of victory.

Firstly, despite their numerical advantage, of the 25,000 French troops, 15,000 of them were mounted knights in full armour. The knights looked magnificent in the pre-battle photos, but with their shiny armour weighing almost 50kg they could actually hardly walk let alone raise their swords in hand-to-hand combat. In fact, you only needed to push one of these overweight French tin-cans over and they instantly became like an up-turned turtle, completely unable to get back on their feet, and left flaying around as if a bee had become trapped under their armour. They were more appropriately dressed for deep-sea diving rather than battle with the far less heavily armoured English.

To make matters worse it had rained almost continuously for 2 weeks, and the recently ploughed land that would serve as the battlefield was actually now just one giant muddy bog. Not only were the French knights hampered by the weight of their armour which already left them puffing like a beached whale, but now having to march through thick mud meant that not only did they move with glacial speed making them easy targets, but by the time they reached the English lines they were already in need of oxygen and about as much use as a helicopter ejector-seat.

The English force on the other hand comprised mainly of archers who carried the uniquely English weapon, the longbow. A trained longbow archer could not only shoot about 6 arrows a minute, the arrows could wound at 400 yards, kill at 200 yards, and penetrate armour at 100 yards. For the English archers, firing at the poor French knights stuck in the mud, out of breath, and flaying around like a middle-aged man on a dance-floor, was like shooting at frogs in a bucket.

The French of course had heard of the longbow, but refused to acknowledge their power, and smugly claimed that when the battle was over they would cut off the index and middle fingers of every archer captured. As an act of defiance the English archers took to taunting the French by sticking two fingers up at them across the battlefield, which to this day remains a peculiarly British gesture of defiance, and which, in the absence of archers, is today mainly confined to football terraces or aimed not quite so defiantly at those in authority when their backs are turned.

The French decision to engage the English at Agincourt was also a strange one. The battlefield was a narrow area of open ground only about half a mile wide flanked on each side by heavily wooded areas. With their overwhelming numerical advantage the French really needed a wide open space so they could flank the English and attack on all sides. But the narrow field of Agincourt only forced the French into a cramped, suffocating formation funnelling all their troops into one narrow corridor, that not only further churned up an already boggy field, but also meant it was difficult for such a large force to manoeuvre effectively, if at all.

Even more surprisingly, the French kept delaying the kick-off time for the battle while their leaders dithered around discussing tactics and whether to wait for even more troops to arrive. Eventually Henry V got fed up waiting, and while the still quite bonkers French King was off discussing military tactics with the trees and flowers, Henry attacked catching the French off guard and unprepared. The French knights lodged an immediate complaint to the match officials stating that this was not accepted protocol but by then it was too late, a hail of arrows from the English longbows was already raining down on them.

The French reacted by attacking the English lines, but the French troops all just got in each other's way, and the situation was made worse as the continuing forward rush of the troops from behind meant that most of the French force spent much of its time face down in the mud having tripped over each other as they tried to move forward.

Those that weren't trampled by horses, or ran into the ever increasing wall of tin that was the French knights hopelessly anchored in the mud ahead of them, were easily picked off by the hail of arrows from the English longbows.

The battle was all but over by lunchtime. Those French soldiers that weren't already dead or still stuck in the mud, fled as the English archers gave them a collective show of two fingers to see them on their way. Approximately 8,000 French lost their lives while Henry had lost less than 500 of his men.

Henry V returned to England hailed as a hero, went on to reconquer Normandy, and by 1419 had reached the gates of Paris. He then entered into a diplomatic marriage to the daughter of the still mad French King and thus became the rightful heir to the French throne. Henry had achieved everything four generations of his ancestors had fought for, he then promptly upped and died.

Henry's heir, the infant Henry VI, was subsequently crowned the King of both England and France, the first and only time the English and French thrones would be united under one King. Unfortunately that one king was a one year old baby, and one who would grow up to be a simpleton who'd eventually go as completely mad as his maternal grandfather. By the end of his reign all of France was once again back in French hands. Oh well.

Regardless, the Battle of Agincourt was to go down as one of the most famous victories in English history, and Henry V was immortalized as the hero king who had seen off the French despite being greatly outnumbered, playing away from home, and with over half his force unavailable due to toiletry issues. The fact that Henry's victory was likely more to do with French incompetence and a couple weeks of particularly wet weather, was quickly glossed over. The French were basically victims of their own arrogance, out-dated tactics, and the fact they were led by a man who thought he could talk to the trees. It would not be the last time.

The English forces at Agincourt were a highly trained, well-paid, professional army, led by a master tactician, and whose use of the longbow meant that the deck was always stacked in their favour. However, England could just as easily have put out an army of farmyard animals and likely the French would still have found a way to lose the battle.

Probably more significantly, the battle served to highlight that men dressed in tin-cans were no longer a viable option as a fighting force when pitted against the longbow, and particularly the soon to be invented musket. Agincourt became the turning point in how battles were fought, and began the steady decline of the age of knights in armour and chivalry. Maidens locked in high towers would now need to think of alternate escape plans, and dragons around Europe let out a collective sigh of relief, but war would never be the same again.

Close, But No China

Christopher Columbus "discovers" the New World

Every year on the second Monday of October, America shuts down its wheels of industry so that everyone can sit on the couch all day to watch football and fill their faces with chips and beer.

The excuse for this day-long annual binge-fest is to allow a thankful nation time to celebrate that pivotal moment in world history when on 12th October, 1492, Christopher Columbus first set foot on a small Island in the Caribbean and thus became forever known as the man who discovered America.

In truth, few people celebrate the day in a way that can even be remotely linked to Columbus. There are no mass gatherings at statues of the great man in every town and city, kids don't dress-up like 15th century explorers in tights and wigs and run around their neighbourhood re-enacting scenes from that historic day, and nobody symbolically plants American flags on their front-lawns. Most modern-day benefactors of Columbus' addition to the world map merely gratefully use the day as an excuse to add to their already sizable waistlines.

The reality is that most Americans came to the realization long ago that Columbus' great "discovery" was actually just the result of a great "mistake" on the part of the revered explorer, and that in fact the vast continents of both North and South America were in fact already populated with several great civilizations who didn't really want or need to be "discovered". They were all quite happily going about their own business long before Columbus stumbled on their homeland thinking he'd actually landed on a different continent altogether still some 5,000 miles further to the west.

In fact, many Americans now see Columbus' inadvertent "discovery" of the Americas as the catalyst for events that would see greed-driven Europeans exploit indigenous civilizations, bringing disease, slavery, and wholesale genocide to people who just had the misfortune to have not yet invented guns, had no immunity to smallpox or yellow fever, and just happened to be sitting on mountains of gold and silver. Although on the plus side, Europeans did ultimately introduce them to soccer, and as for Europe, apart from all that gold and silver, it was now introduced to the culinary joys of potatoes, maize, and tomatoes, and so clearly not all bad news.

However, all told, Columbus' first steps on American soil is probably not the greatest excuse for a nationwide celebration after all, and indeed some States have already renamed Columbus Day as Indigenous People Day to somehow try and redress the balance, while Arkansas has forgone the holiday altogether, although this just adds to the long list of reasons why nobody wants to live there anyway.

So why has Columbus' great voyage of discovery now become almost completely ignored, or at best treated more as a joke and only the result of several mistakes, miscalculations, and stubborn belief, when all the facts clearly pointed to the contrary? Just why did Columbus go from hero to zero, from great discoverer to just a fortunate explorer who just happened to bump into a landmass the size of two continents?

The answer is probably found in the realization that on that fateful October day over 500 years ago, when Columbus heroically set foot on a Caribbean island in the present day Bahamas, Columbus firmly believed that he had actually landed in China, and thus our great explorer clearly had absolutely no idea of where he was at all. The set of criteria for claiming discovery of a whole new continent surely must include actually knowing where you think you are?

Columbus' case is also not helped by the fact that despite three subsequent voyages to the area, exploring numerous islands and interacting with local tribes, he failed to see the significance in the fact that not one person spoke, dressed, or even remotely looked Chinese, and that despite such obvious flaws in his thinking he stubbornly continued to believe right up to the day he died that he had all along been enjoying the sights and sounds of Asia.

It's one of history's great ironies that a man who set off to reach one continent became celebrated for landing on a completely different continent altogether, and then spent the last 16 years of his life mistakenly believing he had reached his original destination all along.

It thus must have come as quite a shock to Columbus on that first day to be fully expecting the Emperor of China to stroll down to the beach to greet him baring buckets of gold as gifts, only to be met by strangely dark-skinned, half-naked natives, carrying only shells and bananas.

But what on earth was Columbus doing cruising around the Caribbean looking for signs of Chinese takeaways and fake handbags anyway, when it was common knowledge that China was to be found east of Europe on the map? Well there was at least a little method in his madness.

China and India were proving to be very profitable trade routes for Europe, but the increasing Muslim domination of the eastern trade routes through the Middle East was making travel to India and China somewhat challenging for the naturally risk-averse European merchants. Having swapped their fortunes for wagon-loads of silk, ivory, and fake handbags, they naturally wanted to ensure they could get them safely home without losing either their precious cargo or their own heads. Thus Columbus hit upon what he thought would not only be a solution to Europe's eastern trade route problem, but also a way to make himself very rich in the process.

Columbus' great idea was that rather than get to India and China by travelling east, why not just go in the other direction and sail west across the Atlantic ocean to get there, and thus by-pass the pesky Muslim hoards altogether. Obviously Columbus wasn't the first to propose the idea, in truth even a three year old child with learning difficulties could probably have come up with it, but it had always been rejected in the past, and for a very simple reason.

By the middle of the 15th century people were now pretty much ok with the idea that the world was actually a sphere and not a flat disc after all, and that you wouldn't fall off the edge of the world if you sailed to far over the horizon. Thus most people understood that if you travelled in a straight line in any direction and just kept going, you'd eventually end up pretty much back where you started.

Similarly then, if you travelled in a straight line in one direction to reach a particular destination, you would also eventually reach the same destination by travelling in the same straight line in the opposite direction. The only issue was the relative distances you had to travel, and this is where the idea of reaching Asia by travelling west had always drawn more laughter than financial backing.

The educated opinion in Columbus' day was that the Earth was a sphere about 24,000 miles in circumference. Therefore, since China was known to be some 8,000 miles to the east of Europe, conventional wisdom held it highly impractical and expensive to sail west for 16,000 miles to reach the same place, regardless of whether marauding Muslim hoards stood in your way or not.

But Columbus was not one to be put off by simple mathematics or conventional wisdom, and so he decided he would come up with his own calculations, which miraculously painted a much different picture as to the westerly distance of Asia from Europe.

By using some obscure mediaeval Persian and Arabic geographers as his reference, and by conveniently ignoring any mathematical logic at all, Columbus somehow managed to re-estimate the circumference of the Earth to be only 18,000 miles, a miscalculation that effectively reduced the planetary waistline down by a whopping 25 percent.

Not content with this little piece of creative number crunching, Columbus then used a few more obscure references, mixed with even more numerical smoke and mirrors, to effectively increase the estimated size of Asia to the point where it stretched eastward to within a stone's throw of Europe.

Happily combining these two errors together, Columbus came to the conclusion that China was only about 3,000 miles to the west of the Canary Islands, a miscalculation of around 60% of the actual distance. Clearly Columbus had the mathematical skills of a goldfish, and naturally faced a great deal of ridicule from those among his contemporaries who had paid a little more attention during class at school, but regardless he somehow managed to convince the King of Spain to finance an expedition for a flotilla of ships to sail west and confirm his fast-track sea route to Asia.

Columbus assumed that Asia could be reached just by pointing his ships west and sailing unimpeded across the Atlantic until he hit Asia. Of course what nobody knew at the time was that there was a rather sizable landmass sitting in between Europe and Asia, putting a rather sizable roadblock in the way of any planned non-stop service straight to Asia. But most importantly, this unknown continent-sized roadblock coincidentally just happened to be right where Columbus and his rather dubious calculations expected to find China.

And so on the 3rd August 1492, Columbus left Spain with 3 large ships, the Santa Maria, the Pinta, and the Niña, several pages of calculations that were about as much use as a chocolate tea-pot, and sailed west towards the sunset, fully expecting to sight the coast of China in a matter of weeks.

Right on cue, after 10 weeks of sailing Columbus sighted land, and setting foot on an island in the present day Bahamas he firmly believed that his calculations had proved correct and that he had landed somewhere on the coast of China. Columbus promptly declared he had arrived in the "Indies", the term used at the time for the region of Asia east of the Indus river, and all he had to do now was fill his ships with gold and sail triumphantly back to Spain a hero.

Unfortunately for Columbus he found no magical land full of riches, no golden palaces, no silk and ivory traders, no noodle shops or markets selling fake handbags and perfume. Much to his surprise Columbus was actually greeted by primitive indigenous natives, half naked, and clearly neither Chinese nor wealthy. But still convinced he was indeed in the Indies, Columbus promptly dubbed these natives 'Indians', and so consigned millions of North and South American indigenous peoples to one of the greatest misnomers in history.

Columbus and his men continued their journey, visiting numerous islands and meeting with the leaders of the native populations who likely just became more and more confused over constant questions around where the Emperor's palace was, and where they were hiding all the silk and gold.

Columbus eventually returned to Spain in 1493, giving glowing and clearly somewhat exaggerated reports about having landed in Asia, and having seen all manner of riches. In the coming years Columbus was to undertake three further expeditions to the Indies further exploring the area, looking for that elusive gold, and somehow convincing himself more and more that he was in Asia despite the complete lack of any evidence to indicate that he was.

In reality, all Columbus really achieved in the Indies was the brutal treatment of the indigenous people, the introduction of slavery, and inciting the near mutiny by the Spanish settlers who were by now coming to realize that they were likely not in Asia at all, and thus unlikely to be getting rich any time soon.

In fact, during Columbus' third expedition word of the ongoing mistreatment reached Spain, and the Spanish Crown felt obliged to send a royal official who promptly arrested Columbus and stripped him of his authority. He returned to Spain red-faced and in chains to face the royal court, used the "it was all just a big misunderstanding" plea and the charges were dropped. But Columbus lost his title as Governor of the Indies and probably a sizable chunk of the riches he had made during his voyages to legal fees.

Christopher Columbus died May 20th 1506, still entirely convinced he had reached Asia. It didn't take long for people to figure out that Columbus' Indies was not Asia at all, and that in fact it was a whole new landmass altogether, one that was collectively referred to now as the "New World". In reality, the closest Columbus had actually ever come to Asia was on a voyage he took as a youth to the Islands of Greece.

Unfortunately, Columbus' real legacy was that within 40 years of his inadvertent "discovery" of the New World, Spanish conquistadors had all but wiped out the rich empires of the Aztec and the Inca, had stripped them of almost every ounce of gold and silver, and paid them back in kind with the introduction of smallpox, yellow fever, and slavery.

The final embarrassment for Columbus was to come several centuries later when archaeologists found evidence of a Norse settlement at Vinland on the northern tip of Newfoundland in modern-day Canada, and dating back to the 11th century. It seems that not only had Columbus not found a route to Asia, he was also not the first European to set foot in the New World either. He was clearly also not very good at maths either.

Friendly Fire Gone Mad

The Battle of Karánsebes

Military top brass will tell you through cold emotionless eyes that friendly-fire, defined as the act of mistakenly attacking a friendly force while attempting to attack the enemy, is an unavoidable reality of war.

They may as well be telling the regular army grunt that not only will the enemy have a virtual target pinned to your chest, but you should also expect that your own comrades will also put one on your back for use as target practice on slow days.

Friendly fire is clearly unacceptable. But there are many recorded cases in recent history that clearly demonstrate that although troops are seemingly well trained in target practice, some additional tutoring on the enemy recognition front may still be needed.

The problem is not helped by the fact that countless armies across the globe all seem to have chosen green for the colour of their uniforms, and just as confusingly, all their top naval brass agreed that grey was the colour all their ships should be painted. The unfortunate result of all this monochromatic military colouring is that from a distance, your brothers-in-arms look exactly the same as the enemy you have been told to shoot on sight.

At the start of every war maybe a quick meeting by the opposing military heads should first be held so sides could choose unique colours for their uniforms and ships. Like soccer teams, armies could also have away-kits for battles on foreign soil, and maybe soldiers could also have their names printed in large letters on their backs for easy recognition to help the colour blind.

However, until Dulux bring out their military combat range, we are left with the unfortunate reality that soldiers need to watch their backs almost as much as what's hiding in the trees ahead of them.

Naturally, military leaders do not want cases of friendly-fire incidents scribbled all across their military records, and so the documented examples of such military ineptitude are probably the just the tip of a very large and embarrassing iceberg. Nonetheless, there are still enough known cases of troops innocently doing the enemy's work for them to understand that this happens more often than a Government U-turn, and often on a larger scale than you'd imagine.

During world War I, at the Battle of Loos in September 1915, the Special Brigade of the British Army, a group of scientific boffins with beards tasked with finding clever and fiendish ways to help the allies overcome the Hun, opened 5,500 cylinders of chlorine releasing 140 tons of gas into the air near the German front-line. Part two of their fiendish plan was unfortunately a little less controllable relying as it did on the wind to then blow the chlorine gas towards German lines, hoping to gas them into surrender.

Unfortunately, a sudden and clearly unexpected shift in the wind direction resulted in the gas being blown back across the British trenches. In addition, retaliatory German artillery fire hit and burst further cylinders of gas, also releasing them into the British lines. The chlorine killed and injured approximately 2000 or more British soldiers. The red-faced boffins of the British Special Brigade were subsequently ordered to attend a 2-day beginners Meteorological course, and then go back to their drawing boards.

In 1917 there was even a reported a case of reciprocal friendly-fire when the British submarine, G9, attacked its fellow British submarine, Pasley, with torpedoes after mistaking it for a German U-Boat. Fortunately Pasley survived the attack, but naturally assuming that they had themselves been fired on by a German U-Boat, Pasley quickly retaliated by ramming G9, all resulting in G9 being cut in half and sinking, leaving only one survivor. Reports later confirmed that the nearest actual German U-boat at the time of the attack was well over 100 miles away.

British submarine Captain's were subsequently reminded to at least give any nearby submarines time to let them know if they were actually fighting on the same side first before engaging, a fairly fundamental point you would have thought, but one that clearly needed repeating.

It also seems that being a high ranking military leader provides no built-in immunity to friendly-fire either. Probably the single most embarrassing case of friendly-fire involving someone who was actually in a position to make decisions was that of Confederate General and wartime superhero Thomas "Stonewall" Jackson.

The American Civil war had already made a hero of General "Stonewall" Jackson, who had made a reputation for himself as a no nonsense, kick-ass leader, with several Confederate victories already on his resume by the time he squared up to face the Union army at the Battle of Chancellorsville in May, 1863, under the leadership of General Robert E. Lee.

Despite the fact that they faced a Union army almost twice their size, the Battle of Chancellorsville was a key victory for the Confederates during the Civil War, due in no small part due to General Lee splitting his troops in half during the battle as a massive confusion tactic, and giving the mighty Stonewall the all-important task of attacking the Union flank with his half the Rebel force.

Stonewall naturally obliged by tearing through the opposition like a hot knife through last week's butter, only stopping his attack because nightfall made it too dark for any effective engagement, and to Jackson's frustration night-vision goggles had not yet been invented.

However, Jackson himself wasn't finished for the day, he was keen to know the Union force's positions so he could be straight out of the blocks and on top of them at first light. But with his typical bravado and arrogance he couldn't wait for any actual intelligence officers to go and gather the information he for him, and announced that he was going to ride out and do the reconnaissance himself.

So out beyond the Confederate lines he rode, accompanied by just a handful of men who quite honestly didn't want to be out at night scouting enemy lines, particularly with someone as gung-ho as Stonewall Jackson. Once their scouting was completed Jackson and his men quickly galloped back to the Confederate lines to prepare for the planned morning attack.

However, at this point Jackson failed to realize one very important point. Your average soldier isn't Stonewall Jackson, or even all that brave, he's cold, and tired, and hungry, and most importantly, he's scared enough to fire at any suspicious movement particularly if said movement is on horseback and riding directly toward him at high speed.

Thus, rather than hearty slaps on the back for their brave act of reconnaissance, Stonewall and his returning party were greeted with panicked gunfire the very second Confederate sentries saw them. The general took three bullets, and subsequently had to have an arm amputated, eventually succumbing to operation-induced pneumonia eight days later. Meanwhile, back at the front-line, several random Confederate sentries wound up with a rather awkward story to tell their commanding officer in the morning.

However, the daddy of all such cases of friendly-fire happened on the night of 17th September 1788, when the Austrian army managed to almost wipe itself out in a friendly-fire incident of such scale that history records the event as a battle all to itself, a battle where uniquely both sides were in fact on the same side.

The Battle of Karánsebes must go down in history as the single greatest example of military ineptitude ever recorded, a battle where almost 100,000 Austrian soldiers mistakenly turned on each other, and by the time all the dust had settled over 10,000 Austrian soldiers were dead or wounded, with the rest left red-faced and with a great deal of explaining to do.

From 1787 to 1791 the then Austrian empire was at war with the Turkish Ottoman Empire primarily in an argument over land that the Ottomans had captured from the Austrians several years earlier, and that the Austrians now decided they wanted back.

In September 1788 the 100,000 strong Austrian army, which at this point was actually made up of a loose amalgamation of Austrian, German, Croat, Serb, Polish, and Italian troops, set up camp around the town of Karánsebes. A contingent of hussars were then dispatched across the nearby Timis river to scout for any sign of lurking Ottoman scouts. The Turks were actually still several days away, and so all the hussars ran into was a band of gypsies who just happened to be in the area selling lucky 4-leaved clovers, and looking for hub-caps to steal.

Never ones to let an opportunity to make money pass them buy, the gypsies promptly sold the hussars several cases of home-brew schnapps, which the hussars then took back to their camp and proceeded to drink, which a few hours later resulted in a rather large contingent of very loud and wobbly horsemen.

A large party of passing foot soldiers soon heard the raucous hussars and decided to gate-crash their party demanding some of the schnapps for themselves. The hussars, who by now were all drunker than an Irish stag party, were in no mood to share their alcohol, and as is usually the case with any testosterone and alcohol mix they didn't express their unwillingness to share with a great deal of tact.

Diplomacy was the first casualty in the ensuing argument which quickly escalated. Swear words in numerous European dialects were exchanged and punches were thrown, and eventually one soldier whose clearly felt his opinion was not being taken seriously enough, fired a shot.

In the ensuing mayhem some bright spark began shouting "Turks! Turks!" which clearly was not helpful at all, and caught unawares and unprepared some soldiers fled the scene in panic, while others got into formation ready for a charge from an imaginary hoard of screaming, heavily mustachioed Turks.

Trying to restore some order one of the Austrian officers shouted "Halt! Halt!" at the fleeing soldiers. Unfortunately the multi-national nature of the troops meant that half of the them understood about as much German as an Amazonian pygmy, and so mistook the pleas for order as cries of "Allah! Allah!", which naturally only served to fuel the chaos.

As the increasingly frantic group of soldiers ran through the camps, an officer reasoned that the charging, shouting men must be the imaginary Turkish attack, and promptly ordered artillery fire. Now awoken by the sound of gun and artillery fire, the entire camp now did what every disciplined soldier would do at a time like this, and they fled firing at every shadow they saw thinking that Turks were over-running the camp. The situation continued to escalate until the army was called into a general retreat from the imaginary enemy.

Two days later the Turkish Ottoman army innocently strolled into Karánsebes to find, much to their surprise, over 10,000 dead and wounded Austrian soldiers. The Turks looked at each other in a delighted yet rather confused "what's happened here?" kind of way, and then once having pieced together what must have happened, fell about the floor in laughter for an hour or so, and then took Karánsebes without having to fire a shot.

Now admittedly, the first recorded account of the events at Karánsebes that night did not appear until 1831, which is over 40 years later, which means that there was plenty of time for the facts to become more than a little skewed. However, even though some of the more learned historians may paint a somewhat different view of the battle, their version of events should be discounted on the grounds that it is nowhere near as funny.

King Loses His Head In Argument Over Tax Return

King Charles I drives England to Civil War

The whole idea of an hereditary monarchy is fundamentally flawed. Yes, it has the benefit of simplicity, one person in sole charge of everything, the government, the economy, and the Church, there is no need for lengthy committees, no time consuming discussion to be had, no differences of opinion to be considered, just the unquestioned decisions of one man with a shiny crown sat on top of his head. Things do get done.

However, there are just a few rather fundamental issues with the idea of an hereditary monarch who wields such absolute power over his country and people. Firstly, the system does make the rather bold assumption that such a person will not only be rather good at managing the country's purse, but will also happen to be the best person to nurture the nation's religious well-being, and by the way will also be pretty nifty at leading an army into battle. A kind of all-in-one, number-crunching priest who doesn't mind spilling the odd drop of blood or two.

To make matters worse, there is no advertising for the role, no "let's find the best man for the job" search, no "Wanted" ads placed in local newspapers. The system just automatically appoints someone whose sole qualification for the job is that his Dad did it before him. Not only that, the lucky appointee also gets to do the job for his entire life regardless of how well or poorly he performs, at which point the job is then just automatically handed over to his eldest son no matter how old or suitable he happens to be. No interview, no background checks, no references, just "can you start on Monday?".

Thus, the real problem with an hereditary monarchy is the shear randomness of the quality of individual the system throws up for what is after all the country's top job. A nation just automatically puts its whole future in the hands of someone who could possibly turn out to be Forrest Gump.

Of course you also guarantee that such a system will likely foster an arrogant and over-protected heir to the throne, a future ruler who has always got everything they wanted, will have never been questioned, criticized, corrected, or had to consider the possibility that they may be wrong. Likely not your most rounded individual then, which means that not only might you get Forrest Gump, you may well get Forrest Gump with an attitude.

Now this all works fine if your monarch turns out to be Alfred the Great, Edward the Confessor, or Richard the Lionheart, but things do start to go a little wrong when your ruler turns out to be either incompetent, mad, or a complete imbecile, or worse of all you find yourself with someone like Charles I.

When Charles became King in March 1625, he was young, arrogant, spoiled, and not the sharpest tack in the toolbox. He believed strongly in a King's divine right to rule without question, and had a nasty habit of having the ears cut off anyone who disagreed with him. He was also very short and had a stammer. So clearly well qualified to be the absolute ruler of both England and Scotland.

Now, with the crown firmly sat on his head, Charles' relationship with Parliament became particularly strained almost from the off. He never quite understood the need for such an institution given his unwavering belief that he had a divine right to rule how he saw fit, and so certainly didn't need a group of pesky politicians telling him who he could or couldn't tax, marry, throw into prison, chop the ears off, or go to war with.

When Parliament refused to grant Charles more money for his ongoing war with Spain, Charles just shrugged his royal shoulders, dissolved parliament for what he saw as its rather presumptuous behaviour, and proceeded to bypass due process altogether and went ahead and raised funds directly via his own understandably unpopular "forced loans".

Under the terms of this innovative "compulsory" lending scheme you were obliged to lend the King large amounts of money or find yourself arrested and spending the next 10 years in prison. Naturally the scheme didn't go down to well with either parliament or the country's now rather less wealthy gentry. Unfortunately, the country was soon to discover that Charles was rather good at inventing creative ways to tax his people, all of which seemed to have a "pay or prison" clause buried in the small print.

Parliament was by now starting to realize they had a sulky adolescent for a king who just threw his toys out of the pram if he didn't get his own way. In a desperate bid to try and restore some order and gain at least a semblance of control over their wayward monarch, Parliament drew up a "Petition of Right" which declared that any taxes that were unauthorized by Parliament were illegal. Still in dire need of funds to support his ongoing tiffs with several foreign powers, Charles was forced to agree to the Petition so making it law, however, he clearly had his fingers crossed behind his back when he signed the document as he then proceeded to take about as much notice of it as a blind pedestrian at a "Do Not Walk" signal.

Eventually by 1629, Charles' patience with Parliament rudely trying to interfere with his "royal prerogative" was now stretched beyond its royal limits, and he simply determined that it would all be so much easier if he just ruled without Parliament altogether. Consequently, Charles dissolved the current sitting of Parliament, and did not call upon Parliament again for another 11 years. So began what historians call the "Eleven years Tyranny" during which Charles gave free reign to how he felt his kingdom should be run, taxed, and governed, blissfully free of any constraints of Parliament, and imprisoning anyone who gave off even the faintest whiff of dissent.

The first order of business was funding, and Charles quickly moved to revive the concept of "Ship money". This was a long since forgotten tax that had historically been levied on ports to pay for naval defences against raiding pirates and foreign invasions. However, in desperate need of money quickly, Charles applied a little more royal creativity and now expanded the "Ship money" tax such that the entire country was now required to pay. On the not unreasonable assumption that an invading fleet was very unlikely to land 100 miles inland from the coast, several landed gentry from the

Shires refused to pay, only to find themselves quickly behind bars, minus their ears, and the tax taken anyway.

Charles of course had also inherited the throne of Scotland, and not content with just fostering resentment and criticism across England, Charles determined to share the love and generously allowed the Scots to also reap the benefits of what was quickly becoming a royal dictatorship.

Charles was no fan of the Scottish Presbyterian faith, or actually anything Scottish at all, and in 1638 he decided to impose his newly commissioned English Prayer Book on the Scottish church without first consulting anyone in a kilt or even remotely Scottish. The Scots, never ones to bottle these things up, duly revolted and marched south to lodge their complaint in a somewhat less than diplomatic manner. Without the support of Parliament, Charles was forced to meet the Scots at Newborn in 1640 with only a hastily formed army of his closest mates, all of who turned out to be useless at fighting and so were soundly beaten, and Charles left facing the embarrassment of the Scots now occupying Newcastle and Durham.

Charles had effectively ruled England without Parliament for 11 years, but now rather embarrassingly with no army and no money to build one, he was finally forced to recall Parliament to help fund his fight against the marauding Scots, in a war where strangely he was, on paper at least, the King of both opposing forces.

It was no surprise to anyone, except of course Charles, that a Parliament still angry about being sent home without pay 11 years earlier was not just going to hand over the keys to the bank vault without first setting a few ground rules. Parliament insisted that Charles first agree a bill that Parliament would be called regularly, that he couldn't just dissolve Parliament on a whim without its consent, that the "Forced Loans" and "Ship Money" were to be abolished, and he'd stop chopping the ears off anyone who disagreed with him.

Charles was backed into a corner and needed money to send the Scots back home over Hadrian's wall, so he tutted, mumbled something under his breath about things not being like this in the old days, and begrudgingly agreed to Parliament's terms. Rather than continue a rather pointless war, the Scots now happily accepted a wagon load of money as payment for their troubles, and then trotted off back to Scotland to buy some whiskey and new kilts.

But then when Irish Catholics also decided to voice their anger by massacring thousands of Protestants colonists, both King and Parliament strangely found themselves in full agreement that an army needed to be raised to quash the rebellion. However, Parliament didn't trust their King with an army all of his own, clearly worried that he would just use this force against them, so they introduced a bill that both the army and the navy should now be controlled by Parliament.

Charles was not best pleased, it was a huge blow to both his powers and his ego, and he did not react well. In response, on the 4th January 1642, Charles threw his "Beginner's Guide to Democracy" book out of the window, and then took 400 soldiers to the House of Commons to arrest the 5 leading Parliamentarians that he saw as the ring-leaders attacking his natural born rights as a king.

This was of course Charles' most insane act to-date. Freedom from arrest in the Houses of Parliament was an historic right for Parliamentarians since the doors to the House had been first opened centuries earlier. To make matters worse for the luckless Charles, the 5 ring-leaders had already been forewarned of his plans and had fled to safety on the other side of town. Charles was left red-faced and now facing open rebellion in the streets of London with citizens seeing this as the final straw in a long list of his abuses of royal power.

Seeing that things were now taking an unfortunate turn for the worse for him in London, Charles quickly raced back to his palace, packed a few essentials, and fled the city with the Crown jewels under his arm and his Queen in tow, and prepared for what was now the inevitable Civil war.

In one more act of lunacy, Charles sent his Queen to the Netherlands to pawn the English Crown jewels to raise money for his army, and then on August 22nd 1642 he raised his standard at Nottingham calling for all Royalist to aid him in his fight against the Parliamentarians. England was now officially plunged into outright Civil war. Seven years later, on 30th January 1649, it would all end rather badly for Charles when the public executioner separated his head from his body, having already lost the war and subsequently been found guilty of high treason and "other offences against the kingdom".

Charles I had inherited the thrones of both England and Scotland at the age of 25. Within the space of just 24 years he had successfully plunged England into an all out civil war that killed almost half of its adult male population, had left England with no ruling monarch and now led by a military dictatorship run by a fanatical puritan named Oliver Cromwell, and to round his short but eventful career off nicely he had also lost his own head.

Fortunately for blue-blooded royalists, Cromwell's puritanical view of how England should be run turned out to be even less palatable than Charles', and once he had effectively closed theatres and pubs, banned Christmas, and outlawed fun, his vision was doomed. The monarchy was re-instated in 1660 with Charles' son, the aptly named Charles II, but thanks to his father's earlier abuses of power and the resulting mayhem, all future monarchs of England and Scotland would now forever be forced to rule with no teeth (metaphorically of course) and with one hand tied behind their back. Although the system of an hereditary monarchy remained, never again would England or Scotland be ruled by a monarch with the power to just chop people's ears off on a whim.

Air-Con, Electric Windows, Exploding Fuel Tank, All Come As Standard

The Pinto, not one of Ford's finest moments

For most of recorded history if you wanted to travel any kind of distance on land you either left two weeks before you needed to be there and walked, or you found yourself a horse. People had tried other cheaper alternatives, but sheep just stopped to eat at the first sign of a patch of grass, cows proved to be no quicker than walking, and pigs just dragged you through every muddy bog they could find and so you only ended up arriving looking and smelling no better than your mode of transport. All three seemed better suited to a dinner plate rather than as an alternative to a trusty nag.

A horse was quick, strong, and far better looking than either a cow, a pig or a sheep. A horse turned any long distance trip from something that required provisions, overnight stops, maps, and several pairs of replacement shoes, into a far more palatable and comfortable day trip.

However, such convenience came at a cost. Horses required feeding, pooped whenever and wherever the mood took them, and most inconveniently of all they tended to die, thus necessitating the need for a string of costly replacements. So even though a horse ticked many of man's transportation boxes, they were still far from ideal.

George Stephenson went someway to trying to solve the issue in 1814 when he invented the steam train, but trains ran to their own timetable and didn't drop you right on the doorstep of where you wanted to go. Once dumped at the nearest train station already two hours late for your meeting, you were still forced to walk the last stretch, and so in many respects you were just back to square one again.

Then, in the late 19th century, some clever bods with enough spare time and money started to build some 4-wheeled contraptions that ran on gasoline, that had enough room to comfortably carry you and a handful of your mates, and would go wherever there was a dirt road to drive them on. These new transportation wonders were called Automobiles, but they were expensive, noisy, and took about a year to build. No one traded in their horse just yet.

Then one day in 1913 a businessman with a keen eye for profit hit on the bright idea to cut both the time and cost of manufacturing cars by building them on an assembly line. Henry Ford had already unleashed his Ford Model T automobile on the American public back in 1908, it was sturdy and reliable, but with a price tag of $850 the average American still needed a sizable lottery win to afford one, and was still way more expensive than either a horse or a good pair of walking shoes.

But by 1913 Henry Ford had opened the first large-scale assembly line factory. As a result the Ford Motor Company was now able to build a new Model T car in just 93 minutes, and probably most importantly of all, was also able to reduce the cost to the American consumer to just $260. Cars were now coming off the assembly lines quicker than bunnies on a rabbit farm, and you didn't have to be J.D. Rockefeller III to afford one. The motor industry never looked back.

But it has not all been one long joyous hug-fest between the increasingly petrol-headed consumer and the ever cost conscious motor industry. For every 4-wheeled, technologically perfect, swimsuit model of a car that rolled off the production lines of the world's auto-makers, there have been as least as many half-arsed loose conglomeration of nuts and bolts that looked like the business end of a camel, that would have the public avoiding car showrooms like the plague.

Not least of which was the 1956 Renault Dauphine. This was a car that had absolutely no redeeming qualities either as a mode of transport or as something to impress the ladies with. It's paper thin construction made it less like an automobile and more like a piece of origami, and stare at it for more than a few minutes and you could actually watch it rust, while its acceleration would have put it at a disadvantage in any drag race involving farm equipment. The fact that the Dauphine sold over 2 million units in France merely proved just how little the French know about cars.

The usually stylish Italians proved no better when in 1984 they gifted the world the motoring disaster that was the 1984 Maserati Biturbo. It didn't take long for the general car buying public to figure out that Biturbo was actually Italian for "Expensive piece of junk" given that everything that could leak, snap, crack, or rupture, did so with alarming regularity, all resulting in its collective Service Advisories creating a file thicker than the collected works of William Shakespeare.

Then there was the mini-craze in the 1970's for 3-wheeler cars such as the Bond Bug and the Reliant Robin, which were really neither one thing or the other. Buy one of these motorized kid's tricycles and you were basically telling the world that not only couldn't you afford a real car, but that you were also too wimpy to ride a motorbike in the wind and the rain. They were flimsy and way too light, and even with your foot hard on the floor if you were facing anything more than a light breeze for a head-wind you quickly found yourself travelling back the way you came. They were about as exciting as ironing. They didn't last long.

However, the most embarrassing automotive hiccup of all time falls firmly in the lap of the company that started it all in the first place, the Ford Motor Company.

In 1970 Ford released the Pinto, a cheap sub-compact car, under the catchy tag-line of "the little carefree car". Sub-compact cars had emerged in the 1960's as a reaction to the new price conscious motorists who no longer had the funds or real-estate to either fuel or park the gas-guzzling cruise-ships on wheels that had been coming out of car showrooms in ever increasing size since the early 50's.

Foreign motor companies like Volkswagen and Toyota had sold millions of these pocket-sized vehicles across Europe, and demand for them was now starting to rise in the United States. Never slow to react to market forces, Lee Iacocca, the then president of Ford Motor Company, decided that Ford would build the Pinto, a sub-compact car which he hoped would ensure Ford quickly cornered the market in the United states, and kept American bums on American car seats.

Iacocca knew that the faster Ford could get the Pinto into production the more market share they could corner, and so he set the boffins at Ford HQ the challenge of getting the Pinto from conception to production in just 25 months, and at a cost to the customer of less than $2,000. Given that the typical timeframe for getting a new car into production was 43 months, Ford's top brains sat and scratched their heads furiously for a while and eventually came to the conclusion that the only way for them to both build a car for that price, and meet such a tight timeline, was for them to cut a few corners here and there. Iacocca nodded his head in agreement, and told them to call him in 25 months when they needed him for the launch photos.

Things went well at first, but then a slightly worrying trend started to appear during the Pinto's testing. It appeared that in rear-end collision tests at over 25 mph, the Pinto had a rather nasty habit of exploding. Clearly worried, the boffins quickly went back to furiously scratching their heads to try and see just what was turning their new sub-compact car into a sub-compact bomb.

Red-faced, the engineers finally advised the board that in their hastily put together and cost constrained design, the walls of the Pinto's fuel tank had been made wafer thin, and the tank then shoved just behind the rear-bumper and right next to a series of protruding bolts.

As a result, in any rear collision with something larger than a shopping trolley and travelling just a little faster than the average glacier, the wafer-thin fuel tank was punctured by the protruding bolts causing a fuel leakage which a spark would then easily ignite, and so quickly turning the Pinto into a weapon of mass destruction. A terrorist explosives expert couldn't have designed it better.

The good news was that the embarrassing flaw had been discovered quickly during testing. The bad news was that due to the compressed 25 month timeframe for delivery, the production lines had already been tooled up to build the Pinto under the current design, rather than waiting for testing to complete as was normal practice.

The Board were now faced with a dilemma. Fix the flaw and be forced to retool the production line which would mean extra expense and missing the 25 month deadline, or ignore the flaw and deliver the Pinto on time. Up to this point it had all been gravy for the Board at Ford, the toughest decision they had had to make in the last 50 years had been whether to leave the toilet seat up or down in the Executive washrooms. But they were now faced with a decision that was causing more than just a few squeaky bums on boardroom seats.

The board decided to call in the number crunchers, and get them to do a cost-benefit analysis weighing up the relative cost of fixing the car's design and subsequent retooling delays, against the expected cost of settling the expected number of lawsuit cases likely to be made against Ford where the Pinto's exploding fuel-tank had turned an average American family into victims of friendly-fire.

Once the boffins had worked their magic, the numbers showed that the cost to fix the Pinto's design would be around $137m, while the cost to settle the expected number of law suits was only going to be around $49m. Greed then quickly replaced common sense, and the board took the decision to remove any reference to "Customer care and safety" from the Pinto's Sales manual, and allow the Pinto to continue under its current design, including the rear-end pyrotechnic surprise. It was cold, it was heartless, but apparently it was good business, and they had the numbers to prove it. It didn't take long for it all to quickly start to unravel.

In May 1972, Lily Gray was driving her shiny new 1972 Ford Pinto with a 13 year old passenger, when the car stalled and was rear ended by another. Upon impact the fuel tank of the Pinto predictably ruptured, leaked fuel, and quickly ignited, killing Lily Gray and severely burning her passenger. The families of the victims understandably started a lawsuit against the Ford Motor Company.

Their lawyers sent out an army of Erin Brockovich types to see what they could dig up about the Pinto, and it didn't take long before Ford's cost benefit-analysis of the Pinto flaw, what became known as the "Pinto memo", turned up as Exhibit A in the subsequent court case. The family's lawyers gleefully relieved themselves all over Ford's now non-existent defence.

What made matters worse was that the now infamous "Pinto memo" not only highlighted Ford's "profits above life" approach, but it also became clear that in their calculations Ford had used a shockingly low value for what it felt was the value of a human life, a mere $200,000. Which, if you allow for inflation, bank charges, exchange rates, lawyer fees, and the price of an ice-cream on the way home, meant that Ford actually valued their customer's lives at not much more than the cost of the car that had just abruptly ended that life.

And just to add a little more vinegar to Ford's cocktail of shame, the memo also revealed that the estimated cost for Ford to have fixed the Pinto issue was a mere $11 per car. Ultimately, Ford had preferred to sell a known ticking-bomb to its customers rather than spend $11 to defuse it. Ford had been caught not only with its pants down, but with its private memos flapping in the wind.

Several of Ford's top designers were fired as a consequence of the whole debacle, but who apparently did go on to enjoy surprisingly successful careers in the Explosives Research Department of the U.S. military. As for Ford's board members who had actually made the decision to approve the Pinto's explosive, non-optional extra, they all developed Teflon suits overnight and survived with their high-paid jobs intact. Before the Pinto was finally pulled from the market, 27 people were determined to have been killed in rear-end crash explosions involving Pintos, and the Ford Motor Company lost untold millions in compensation claims. Ford's reputation was also put on life-support which no end of cost-benefit analysis could fix.

The world assumed that the motor industry as a whole had learned its lesson. But maybe not. In 1975 the Morgan Motor Company in England managed to manoeuvre its way around some rather prohibitive U.S. emissions and safety requirements by getting their latest model certified to run on propane gas. It was a novel idea, and the company was applauded for its innovation, but quickly raised a few eyebrows when the first of the Morgan Plus 8 Propane vehicles rolled out of the factory sporting tanks of liquid propane hung perilously behind the rear bumper. Fire-proof seat covers were generously offered as an optional extra, but no word yet on whether any cost-benefit analysis was requested by the Morgan board. However, lawyers remain on stand-by.

Spanish Invasion Fails Due To Lack Of Weather Report

Bad planning and weather defeats the Spanish Armada

The reign of Queen Elizabeth I of England during the second half of the 15th century was a difficult time for the then King of Spain, Philip II. At the time Philip was, on paper at least, the most powerful monarch in Europe and had been pushing his Catholic agenda to anyone who would listen and could understand his accent.

Philip thought he had already dealt with the pesky little Island on the other side of the English channel when in 1554 he married the then English Queen, Mary I, the Catholic daughter of Henry VIII and Catherine of Aragon. As part of the wedding package Philip enjoyed Mary's titles and honours and was able to co-reign over England for as long as they remained married. As a consequence of the rather messy divorce between Mary's parents, England was a country that was now somewhat outside of Rome's sphere of influence and Philip seized the opportunity to help Mary push her own Catholic agenda, although in truth, "Bloody Mary" needed little encouragement with this particular task given that she was already burning at the stake anyone she saw without rosary beads or a life-size poster of the Pope in their living-room.

It was all going rather swimmingly for Philip, and then unfortunately Mary upped and died which presented Philip with a bit of a problem given that their marriage had not yet produced any suitable heir to the throne, and his master plan to return England to the Catholic fold was still very much a work in progress. Mary's death meant that Philip now lost his power and influence over England's top job, and to make matters worse the next in line to the throne was the decidedly Protestant Elizabeth, Henry VIII's other surviving daughter.

In a desperate plan to hold on to some level of influence over England, Philip hastily sent a proposal of marriage to his ex-sister-in-law, the now Queen Elizabeth I. But clearly unimpressed by his Mediterranean charm and promises of cheap holidays on the Costa del Sol, she refused him, leaving Philip somewhat red-faced and also now with a corner of Europe where the pendulum was quickly swinging back to the Protestant side of the religious spectrum.

Matters got worse when Philip's one remaining ally on British soil, the Catholic Mary Queen of Scots, fled south to England in 1568 after being implicated in the murder of her second husband by her now third husband. It was all very messy, and Elizabeth was forced to imprison Mary while an enquiry into her alleged wrong doings and the paperwork for extradition orders back to Scotland were completed. However, while in prison Mary was also implicated in a subsequent plot to murder Elizabeth and have herself declared Queen and thus restoring a Catholic to the throne.

Clearly, Mary now had to go, and her execution in 1587 upset the Catholic crown heads of Europe, and particularly Philip II of Spain who now saw his hopes of placing a Catholic on the English throne going the same way as his earlier marriage proposal to Elizabeth.

Elizabeth was also causing Philip a few problems a little closer to home. She was quietly supporting Protestants in the then Spanish owned Netherlands, who themselves were already pushing for less flamenco dancing and paella, and more clogs and windmills. In addition, under Elizabeth's direction, Sir Francis Drake and his sailing buddies had been attacking Spanish shipping in the West Indies which resulted in Spain losing vast sums of money to what Philip considered to be English "pirates".

By 1586 Philip had just about had enough of Elizabeth, England, and Protestants as a whole. He had tried to solve the problem by diplomacy and even by marriage, but such soft-touch approaches had got him nowhere, and so Philip now decided that a somewhat more direct approach was needed. With a bold but somewhat vague idea around knocking Queen Liz off of her throne and triumphantly returning England to Catholicism, Philip gathered his trusted leaders and boldly announced that he planned to invade England.

Philip's plan was to build a huge Armada of ships, fill them to the rafters with guns and soldiers, sail up the English channel, land somewhere on the coast of England, march to London, depose

Elizabeth, and celebrate with a Catholic Mass at Westminster Abbey before returning home to Spain with the English crown safely tucked away in his hand luggage.

But Philip's hastily drawn up invasion plan had more holes in it than a Swiss cheese and was in trouble even before the amassed ships left port. The man first assigned to lead the great Armada was the highly experienced naval commander the Marquis of Santa Cruz, who gratefully accepted the job but then promptly died. Philip then appointed the Duke of Medina Sidonia, an administrator who was a particular court favourite but who had little military experience on either land or sea, was in poor health, and who suffered from acute sea-sea-sickness.

In addition, in the haste to ready the Armada the water and provisions for the ships were stored in barrels freshly made of new wood, wood that was still damp, and so within a matter of days the food began to rot and the water became a deadly cocktail of mould and bacteria.

Regardless, with great fanfare the Spanish Armada sailed from Spain in July 1588 with 130 ships, 8,000 sailors, and 18,000 soldiers all ready to invade England. At its head was a seasick pen-pusher with a less than well thought out invasion plan in his back pocket, and on each ship the stores were quietly turning into manure. Meanwhile Philip, confident of success, went back to his palace to pick out a new colour scheme for Windsor Castle.

Initially all went according to plan, the Armada sailed towards the English channel in a crescent-shaped battle formation which offered the fleet the best protection, and indeed the Armada had faced little opposition to speak of by the time it reached the coast of Cornwall at the end of July. However Elizabeth was well aware that Philip had gone off the deep-end and was likely to mount a less than diplomatic offence on her throne, and so had beacons set up all along the English coast and up to London which could be lit to send a warning message as soon as any invading fleet was spotted. Fortunately it wasn't raining, and no one manning any of the beacons had fallen asleep or forgotten their box of matches, and so within a day of the Armada reaching Cornwall, London was aware of the threat and readied itself.

The appointed head of the English fleet, Sir Francis Drake, was playing bowls in Plymouth when he was informed that the English Channel was quickly filling up with Spanish tourists none of who looked like they were coming over for a quiet weekend of sightseeing. Unworried by either the size or proximity of the Armada, Drake insisted he still had time to first finishing his game of bowls before needing to strap on his armour and heading off down to the docks to set sail to meet the Spanish invaders.

In reality all the while the Armada stayed in its cunning crescent-shaped formation there was little Drake or his ships could do anyway. Effectively, as the mighty Armada sailed up the English Channel the attacks by Drake's Plymouth fleet proved mostly ineffective and nothing more than an annoying distraction that kept the Spanish sailors from their usual afternoon siestas.

It was all going rather well for Medina Sidonia at this point, but it was now that the next big flaw in the Spanish plan became blindingly apparent. Medina Sidonia had orders to take the Armada to the Netherlands where it was to pick up another 30,000 crack soldiers who were ready and waiting to join the invasion. Unfortunately, Medina Sidonia quickly discovered that there was actually no port deep enough on the Netherlands coast to harbour his fleet.

At this point Medina Sidonia made a note in his journal in big bold letters to remind himself to talk to the invasion planners on his return to Spain, and then set about looking for the nearest harbour that was actually deep enough to moor his fleet. Unfortunately that harbour turned out to be Gravelines near Calais, a few hundred miles away from where the crack troops were sat waiting twiddling their thumbs.

A few days later a less than happy Medina Sidonia parked his Armada at Gravelines, wrote an apologetic letter to the Duke of Parma who was at the head of the 30,000 troops still waiting back in the Netherlands advising him that unfortunately if he wanted to take any part in the planned invasion of England he and his troops would now first have to make their way over to Calais. He attached the local bus and train timetable, and then sat down to wait for the troops to arrive and wondered just what could go wrong next.

For his part, Drake was in desperate need of a lucky break, both literally in the defensive crescent-shaped formation of the Armada, and figuratively, and seeing the Armada now docked at Gravelines he sniffed an opportunity. Drake came up with the rather cunning plan to take a handful of his older ships, load them up with oil, wood, lat week's newspapers, any unwanted unpaid bills, and anything else he could find that would burn well, set fire to them and then gently push them in the general direction of the resting Armada.

The ships of the Armada were all made of wood and with canvas sails, and were themselves fully loaded with gunpowder, if they all caught fire the resulting explosion would likely be heard back in Spain. Thus, as the Armada saw the burning ships approaching, panic quickly replaced order, ships broke their moorings and attempted to break out of Gravelines to save themselves. Only one Spanish ship was actually lost to the burning English ships but in the panic the Armada's crescent shape had been broken and it was now vulnerable to attack.

Drake seized his chance and attacked, but they were bravely fought off by the Spanish who by now had recovered their composure, and at this point the Armada was still fairly intact to fight another day. In military terms the engagement in the English channel had not been much more than a tactical draw. However, the English fleet by now had blocked off any chance the Armada had of going back down the English Channel, and by the time the Armada reassembled back into its defensive shape, Medina Sidonia found the only course left open to him was to go up the east coast of England around the north of Scotland, past the western Irish coast and then back to Spain.

It was at this point that Medina Sidonia realized he should have paid a little more attention to the long-range weather forecast before he left Spain as the Armada now sailed straight into the eye of one of the fiercest hurricanes recorded around the northern British Isles. To make matters worse the rotting food and water in the ship's stores now meant that the Armada supplies were not enough to make the journey back to Spain with the expected 3 square meals a day.

Within days half the ships in the now starving Armada were being driven onto the rocks of Scotland and Ireland by the storm. Only 67 ships out of the original 130 managed to limp back to Spain, and over 20,000 Spanish sailors and soldiers were lost, most of the damage having been inflicted by starvation and Scottish and Irish rocks rather than any English cannon. For their own part, the English had lost only a 100 men and a handful of ships which they had set fire to themselves anyway and so they didn't really count.

Had the Armada succeeded and landed its 50,000 battle-hardened Spanish troops with their buckets and spades somewhere on the beaches of Kent, it's very likely they would have been in the streets of London within a matter of days. Within a couple of months England would have reverted back to the Catholic faith, bull-fighting rings would have sprung up in every major town, and everyone would now be speaking Spanish as they ordered their Tapas and Chips.

English history books record events as a huge victory for Elizabeth, beating the might of the Spanish Armada with just a few rowing boats, a couple of big sticks, and some plucky English spirit. The truth however is that Elizabeth could probably just as easily have sent out a handful of pensioners in pedelos and the Armada would still have failed. At the end of the day the failure of the Armada was much more to do with Spanish bad planning and a couple of unseasonably rainy days around the north coast of Britain, rather than any English ingenuity or plucky fighting spirit.

But, England's seemingly miraculous deliverance from mighty Catholic Spain secured the reputation of Elizabeth I, giving her an heroic status, and set in motion the emergence of England as master of the seas, and ensured it would very soon be forcing half the world to speak English and drive on the left-side of the road.

As for Spain, the embarrassment of the failed Armada was the catalyst for its decline as Europe's super power, and ultimately forced it to settle for the rather lesser role as Europe's top destination for cheap package-holidays and timeshare homes.

Big Trouble At Little Big Horn

General Custer's Last Stand

On June 25th, 1876, the 7th Cavalry Regiment of the United States Army under the command of Lieutenant Colonel George Armstrong Custer, decided to pick a fight with a rather large force of Native American tribes led by Chief Sitting Bull, at what became known as the Battle of the Little Bighorn, in the eastern Montana territory of the United States. By the time all the dust had settled the U.S. 7th cavalry had been all but wiped out, with five companies completed annihilated, including Custer himself, and Sitting Bull was happily leading 10,000 Cheyenne, Lakota, and Arapahoe warriors in a victory dance.

On the scorecard of the ongoing Indian wars it would not be marked down as a particularly great day for the U.S. army, yet the battle was to provide one of the most universal and enduring legends of all time. The story of the dashingly handsome, golden-haired, buckskin-wearing Custer, bravely fighting off native savages while hopelessly outnumbered, out of bullets, with one hand holding up the American flag and the other fighting off countless savages, is the stuff of legend and boyhood heroes. It was the original textbook all-American hero going out in a blaze of glory.

No other single event in American history has captured the public's imagination more completely. Custer's "Last Stand" is etched into America's soul as one of the most iconic events of the romantic old West and has subsequently become the topic of over 300 books, 50 movies, and 1,000's of paintings. And at its centre is George Armstrong Custer, the all-American super-hero, who if he had a cape and wore his underpants on the outside of his trousers history would likely have also recorded that he had x-ray vision and flew faster than a speeding bullet.

But the truth, it seems, was rather different. Evidence now shows that the massacre of the 7th Cavalry at the Little Big Horn may well have been more due to incompetence, arrogance, and a series of school-boy tactical errors made on the part of Custer, which led to more of an embarrassing and disorganized rout, rather than any heroic "Last Stand" against overwhelming odds. It seems that actually all the Indians needed to do to post the win was just turn up.

In fact from the outset there was always a bit of a mismatch between Custer the heroic craggy-faced all action Marlboro-man, and Custer the reality. Custer had actually graduated last in his class from West Point in June 1861, and then just a few days after graduating, he failed as officer of the guard to prevent a fight between two cadets and faced a court-martial, only to be saved by the outbreak of the Civil War and the desperate need for officers. Fortunately for Custer, for any army in the midst of a the Civil war, any officer was better than no officer at all.

Custer did however prove a daring and brave leader throughout the American Civil war, leading his Union Army men to several famous victories. But while Custer may have been brave, he was also reckless, an impetuous and vain romantic, and a shameless self-promoter, whose ego meant he ignored orders and took appalling risks with his men's lives, seemingly more concerned with a good photo opportunity and making the front pages of the newspapers than his or their safety.

By all accounts he was also disliked by his men, so much so that at one point over 80 men under Custer's command deserted after taking a vote where they collectively agreed that their glorious leader was actually nothing more than a vain dandy, and that their odds of living beyond the next few weeks would be decidedly improved even as deserters, rather than under Custer's command.

Yet the U.S. Army top-brass loved him, they needed a hero the American people could look up to, and Custer was more than willing to play the role. The press gushed over the heroic deeds of the young, bright, golden-haired, long-locked Custer, fighting for the glory of his regiment, and wearing red neckties onto the battlefield so that everyone, including the photographer, knew exactly who he was.

Within a short space of time the nation's favourite action-man had been promoted to Lieutenant Colonel, later being given the honorary title of Brigadier General, and in September 1868 Custer was given the command of the newly formed 7th Cavalry. The dashing

"General" Custer, a man who could seemingly ride, shoot, drink, polish his boots, and pose for a photograph all at the same time, was now about to be thrust into the middle of the Indian wars.

Lakota Chiefs Sitting Bull and Crazy Horse had been successfully resisting American efforts to confine their people to reservations for more than a decade. But the growing tide of white settlers getting in the way of their annual buffalo hunts had led to some rather robust "discussions", and in 1875, when the U.S. Army blatantly ignored treaty provisions and trampled their army boots all over their sacred Black Hills, Sitting Bull had finally had enough.

The aging Chief promptly put out his Peace-pipe and sent out smoke-signals to all the other tribes in the area to stop playing nice with the "pale-faces", slap on a new coat of war-paint, and join him in Montana to settle the issue once and for all. By the late spring of 1876 more than 10,000 Indians from the Cheyenne, Lakota, and Arapahoe tribes had gathered in a massive camp along a river in southern Montana called the Little Big Horn.

At around the same time, acting on typically poor military intelligence, the 600 men of the 7th Cavalry under the command of Lieutenant Colonel George Armstrong Custer were sent out to scout for signs of a large Indian encampment of what was believed to hold up to 800 renegade Lakota Indians gathering in Montana. Unbeknown to Custer, Sitting Bull was actually breaking all known "pow-wow" attendance records at the Little Big Horn with a force over 10 times that size.

To make matters worse, with typical arrogance Custer had refused the offer of an additional battalion of men from the 2nd cavalry, stating that his own 7th cavalry could handle anything Sitting Bull could throw at them. In addition, although his men were only issued with single-shot Springfield rifles, Custer also refused to take along a battery of horse-drawn Gatling guns that could fire up to 350 rounds a minute, believing that the large field guns would only slow him down. Custer was clearly keen to once again make the front pages of the newspapers before anyone else could steal his thunder.

It appears then that Custer marched off to Montana fully expecting to find and engage an Indian force of only around 800 strong, a force that he believed was just a screaming hoard of half-naked savages, and who had only bows and arrows, axes, and large sticks to fight with. Custer's plan was to find Sitting Bull and his band of stone-age warriors, quickly score yet another famous victory, and be home in time to read all about it in the morning papers.

Unfortunately for Custer, he didn't know that Sitting Bull had also recently been down to his local Guns & Ammo Superstore and purchased several wagon-loads of Winchester repeating rifles and buckets full of ammo. Not only did Sitting Bull have a much larger force, they were also now better armed than Custer's 7th cavalry. Custer was marching straight into something of a military nightmare.

Custer force-marched his men 30 miles a day until they finally arrived just east of the Little Big Horn river on the evening of June 24th 1876, exhausted, hungry, and more ready to put their feet up for a couple of days than battle with some 10,000 or so rather disgruntled Indians.

At sunrise the next day Custer's scouts reported they had spotted a gigantic Indian village two miles long and a quarter of a mile wide with thousands Indian warriors who were clearly not there for a local craft fair. There were probably more Indians than the troopers had bullets in their belts which is never a good sign, but in the first of his mistakes that day Custer seems to have assumed that his scouts were simply unable to count properly, and he dismissed their claims as a whiskey-fuelled exaggeration.

Then, ignoring his orders to wait for reinforcements, the fact that his men were already half dead from exhaustion, and fearing that the Indian force would scatter once his presence was discovered and rob him of a chance for glory and the perfect photo-op, Custer decided that he would attack the Indian encampment without delay.

Custer then made what was to turn out to be a series of further tactical errors that probably helped explain why he finished last in his class at West Point. First he ordered Captain Fredrick Benteen to take three of the regiment's 12 companies on a reconnaissance mission to scout the area more thoroughly, however this merely reduced Custer's already badly outnumbered fighting force by 25 per cent. He then ordered Captain Thomas McDougall to take one company to go and escort the slower moving supply train carrying their provisions. Custer's fighting force was now down by a third, and his already slim odds of victory were now edging slowly closer to zero. At this point you would have got better odds on another virgin birth than Custer ending the day in victory.

But Custer didn't stop there. He then ordered his Second-in-command, Major Marcus Reno, to take three more companies and ride down the left bank of a tributary of the Little Bighorn river and engage with the Sitting Bull's force from the south. Custer would then lead the remaining five companies, 215 men, down the right and engage Sitting Bull from the north. Sitting Bull was probably watching all this from the comfort of his Tee-pee thinking that last night's war-dance was clearly paying off.

Custer's 7th Cavalry was now hopelessly divided and about to quickly discover that Sitting Bull had a significantly larger, and far better equipped force than Custer had reckoned on. The first to come to this realization was Reno, who engaged the Indian camp while Custer moved his men northward.

Suddenly faced with the stark realization that rather than engaging just a few hundred stick wielding savages, he was actually now facing thousands of rifle-carrying warriors hell-bent on separating his hair from his head, Reno did what any red-blooded soldier would do and he quickly turned on his heels and ran back to the relative safety of the bluff on the other side of the river. Fortunately for Reno, he was met there by Benteen's returning scouting detachment who arrived just in time to save Reno's men from their own likely massacre.

As he made his own way northward along the Little Big Horn river with his 5 companies of men, it also slowly began to dawn on Custer that his scouts probably could count after all, and that he was now hopelessly detached from the rest of his regiment and facing a significant force of Indians carrying weapons decidedly more late 19th century than he'd expected.

Custer immediately dispatched urgent orders in an attempt to regroup his regiment, but Reno and Benteen were busy dodging bullets at the other end of the Indian camp and were unable to come to the aid of their glorious leader.

Soon, Custer and his 215 men found themselves hopelessly cut off and under attack by as many as 3,000 armed braves. In less than the time it takes to spoil your underwear and say a few last minute prayers they were wiped out to the last man. The remaining battalions under Reno and Benteen were also badly beaten, but they managed to fight a holding action until the Indians withdrew the following day when army reinforcements arrived.

Modern-day analysis of the site where Custer and his men made their "Last Stand" suggest that rather than being surrounded and fighting on heroically against the overwhelming odds, they were simply overwhelmed by a single Indian charge with the surviving soldiers merely fleeing in panic in all directions.

News of Custer's demise at the Little Big Horn was met first with disbelief and then anger, and resulted in the U.S. government taking a far tougher stance on the Native American people. Given that not one soldier had survived to tell the tale of what had actually happened, people just naturally assumed that there must have been some foul-play or trickery on the part of Sitting Bull to result in the massacre of an entire force under the command of such an heroic leader. Clearly it wasn't Custer's fault, Sitting Bull had cheated.

Thus the legend of Custer and his heroic last stand grew, and grew, and somehow everyone managed to just ignore the fact that George Armstrong Custer was just an arrogant, superior, obsessive egomaniac who had finally over-reached himself at the Battle of the Little Big Horn. But apparently he did have great hair, so that's OK then.

If You Go Down To The Woods Today You're Sure Of A Big Surprise...

The Roman Varian disaster

By the time Jesus of Nazareth was playing his one-man miracle show to sell-out crowds in amphitheatres across the Holy land, the Roman Empire had already ruled over most of Europe, North Africa, and East Asia for as long as anyone could remember.

It had all been rather easy to that point. Only Hannibal had seriously threatened the mighty Roman machine when he surprised everyone by coming over the Alps with his army and a dozen or so elephants some 200 years earlier, while the Scots were deemed so mad that rather than deal with them head-on Rome preferred to just build a big a wall to keep them out. But just about everyone else within a few thousand mile radius of Rome was by now counting using letters instead of numbers, speaking Latin, wearing togas, attending orgies on Saturdays, and feeding Christians to lions on Sundays.

Even the usually volatile barbarian tribes of Germania, east of the Rhine, had bowed to Rome's power with a series of uneasy alliances based mostly around some loose agreements that they wouldn't attack any Roman settlements as long as the Romans stopped laughing at their silly accents and their worrying habit of going into battle naked.

To this point it was pretty much the case that if the Roman top-brass sitting back in Rome saw a piece of the world map that took their fancy, they merely sent in their feared Roman legions who usually had all the towns in the area renamed in Latin within a few weeks of their arrival. Roman legions were ruthless, efficient, and were pretty much undefeated, just the sight of them coming over the hill was usually enough for most barbarian tribes to turn around and politely bend over. But all that was shortly about to change.

Around 10 B.C., clearly fed up with the idea of having to keep fighting naked barbarians with strange German accents, Rome sent the full force of its army east across the Rhine to finally bring the local barbarian tribes under its rule. One such tribe was the Cherusci, who now quickly realized that being an ally of Rome was going to be far less detrimental to their health than being its enemy, and so soon became Rome's new best friend.

However, the Romans clearly had underlying trust issues as they made it a habit of taking the eldest son of any new tribal ally as a hostage to ensure their continued obedience, but also to ensure the future tribal king was brought up as a somewhat more civilized Roman, and thus far less likely to cause Rome any trouble once his Romanized royal-rear was sat on his throne.

Thus, Gaius Julius Arminius, the young son of the Cheruscan chief, was taken to Rome, received a military education, and subsequently demonstrated such intelligence and aptitude that he was eventually trained to become a Roman military commander.

By 6 A.D. the Romans believed the land they called Germania was now all but conquered. What they needed now was to send in someone to bring a little Roman civilization to the newly conquered people, or at least get their warriors to put some clothes on. The man Rome chose to bring some much needed culture and dress sense to the new Roman province of Germania was Publius Quinctilius Varus.

Varus had recently served as Governor of Syria, where his style of administration had proved to be less about winning the hearts and minds of the people and more about exercising his passion for crucifixions. Varus was a cruel administrator who specialist subject was brutally subjugating an already subjugated people, and he wasted no time demonstrating his particular style of administration to the people of Germania.

With his homeland now presumed safely under the ruthlessly efficient Varus, Arminius was now free to return home where he became a trusted advisor to the new Governor who was happily picking up just where he left off in Syria, and sweeping the polls as the least popular man in Germania. But unbeknown to Varus, Arminius had returned home with a plan.

It turns out that Arminius had never really embraced the Roman idea of civilization, seemingly being not that fond of orgies, feeding Christians to lions, or wearing togas. Arminius had always believed that the tribes of Germania should be free to rule themselves, including being free to fight buck-naked if they wanted to. Arminius it seems dreamed of uniting the tribes of Germania, freeing themselves of Rome, and setting up an independent empire all of their own, and of course one naturally ruled by a King who would coincidentally just happen to be called Arminius.

In fact, even before Arminius returned to Germania, Rome was already unknowingly playing straight into his hands. Firstly Rome had just spent the last 20 years or so training the wannabe King of Germania in all the skills, tactics, and techniques of the Roman legions. Arminius had memorized the legionnaires' playbook, and knew exactly how the seemingly unbeatable Roman army could indeed be beaten.

Arminius' lofty plans were also helped by the fact that Rome had sent a pen-pusher to rule over Germania, rather than a military leader who might at least have a clue as to how to handle a local rebellion with something other than a strongly worded letter to cease and desist. The mighty Roman legions in Germania were now currently being run by an accountant.

It was of course also a huge bonus for Arminius that the accountant in question was not only useless as a military leader, but also cruel and vindictive. It made the job of convincing the various tribes to join Arminius in rebellion something of an easy sell. The choice between signing up to help create your own country, or run the daily risk of crucifixion just because you forgot to turn up to sword practice without your pants on, is a relatively easy one.

By 9 A.D., Arminius had successfully forged a secret alliance of Germanic tribes and began to plan for rebellion. Arminius' plan was a simple one, as a dutiful advisor to Varus he would report a fictitious "uprising" that needed the resident Roman legions to help quickly squash, he would then lead them straight into quite possibly the biggest ambush of all time.

And so, having lined all his Germanic ducks up in a nice neat row, Arminius approached Varus and advised him that he had got wind of a local uprising which he felt needed to be dealt with urgently. Varus panicked, agreed, then ordered his 3 legions of crack Roman soldiers to prepare to put down a few local tribes who had now seemingly grown ideas above their station. Varus had spent his life either shuffling paper or crucifying people, so clearly he wouldn't have recognized a trap even if it jumped up and bit him on his ample behind, which is exactly what this one was about to do.

By September of 9 AD, Varus had crunched the numbers and felt confident of a quick victory. Varus personally led his three full legions of Rome's finest troops, a total of nearly 15,000 legionaries, and set off to find and destroy the rebellious tribal alliance, guided by the man he thought was his trusted advisor, but who was actually the leader of the very rebellion he was aiming to squash. If gullibility was measured by distance, Varus' would have stretched all the way back to Rome.

As part of his cunning plan Arminius led the long, winding column of Roman legions straight into the dense, thick, and very muddy Teutoburg Forest in North West Germany where the collective might of his naked Germanic warriors were hiding ready to jump out and shout "Boo!".

As Arminius pulled the unsuspecting Legions deeper and deeper into the forest the line of Roman troops, which was already seven or eight miles long when it set off, now became dangerously stretched out over almost 20 miles of the dense forest. Varus' Roman Legions were now marching almost in single-file along narrow muddy forest tracks and bogs, they were by now extremely vulnerable to attack and unknowingly marching straight into quite possibly the biggest ambush in recorded history. A coach party of pensioners from the local old people's home could probably now have picked them off one-by-one without so much as a flutter from their pacemakers.

Despite having his Roman legions now stretched out like a rubber band it seems that Varus still failed to smell a rat, but even he must have become just a little suspicious when Arminius then announced that he needed to be excused from duty for a while to go and deal with some urgent personal business that had just come up. Once free of Roman eyes, Arminius joined his German buddies already hiding in the forest, swapped his Roman Away-team kit for his Germania Home-team kit, switched from Latin to something a little more Germanic, and then immediately launched a series of attacks on the unsuspecting Roman Legions.

Little by little, individual sections of the 20 mile long Roman column were surprised, jumped upon, broken, and surrounded before the Romans could respond. The Roman horsemen were next to useless in the muddy bogs and narrow trails, the Roman archers hardly had time to aim between all the trees at an enemy who simply melted back into the forests after each attack, while the massive numbers of the Roman column made movement in the dense forest trails highly restrictive, and just added to all the confusion. It was effectively a Roman turkey shoot.

In the space of just three days, the alliance of Germanic tribes annihilated all three Roman legions commanded by Governor Varus who, in a rare act for an accountant, fell on his own sword rather than be captured and forced to do the local tribe's books. Nearly 15,000 elite Roman soldiers had died at the hands of people they regarded as barbarians, and who were led by a man they had regarded as a friend.

In total, more than 10 percent of the entire imperial Roman army had been wiped out in one fell swoop, and the myth of its invincibility was shattered. Rome of course blamed everything but themselves for the debacle, they blamed the sunshine, they blamed the moonlight, and they even blamed the boogie. But regardless, their mighty Roman soldiers, once universally seen as bullet proof and able to bench-press tree-trunks, were now seen more as gullible fools who fought like girls with handbags. All in all, it was not a great couple for days for Rome, or accountants.

Of course Roman retribution quickly followed, and over the course of the next seven years Rome fought a series of merciless campaigns that ultimately defeated Arminius' forces. But the damage had been done, Rome's all-conquering mindset had been halted by some naked Germans, the battle abruptly ended the period of triumphant Roman expansion, and most importantly it was to prove a decisive moment in the development of Europe.

Rather than risk any future embarrassment against angry German hoards, Rome decided to confine itself to the area of relative safety west of the Rhine, and left everything on the other side of the river well alone for the next 400 years. Rome never again attempted to conquer Germanic territory east of the Rhine River, either with or without an accountant.

Had Rome not been defeated and pulled its empire back to the Rhine, a very different Europe would have emerged. Almost all of modern Europe would have likely come under Roman rule, and thus there would have been no boundary created between Germanic and Latin cultures which lasts to this day. There would have been no Beethoven, no Einstein, no BMW or Mercedes, no Protestant Reformation, no House of Habsburg, no 30 year war to tear Europe apart, no frankfurters, no arguments over early morning towels on sun-beds, and no German national soccer team to continually beat England on penalties.

Needless to say, Arminius and the battle of the Teutoburg Forest was eventually used to foster the idea of German nationalism. After what we can only assume was some pretty intense lobbying by the German Comedy Guild, Arminius' name was eventually changed to Hermann, and "Hermann the German" became seen as the liberator of Germany, its first national hero, and a central figure in German nationalistic propaganda, not least by a short angry man named Adolf, who sported a very strange looking moustache, and who had his own eyes on Germany ruling all of Europe. Varus it seems has a great deal to answer for.

Fidel Castro Proves He's Indestructible

The Bay of Pigs invasion

On January 1st, 1959, a young Cuban nationalist named Fidel Castro drove his guerrilla army into Havana and politely advised the nation's American-backed president, General Fulgencio Batista, that now would probably be a good time for him to resign. Batista looked out the window of his presidential palace, saw Castro's tanks pointing in his general direction, packed his bags and left, never to return, leaving Castro to assume military and political power.

Once he'd unpacked his books, clothes, and cigars, Castro immediately took steps to reduce American influence on the island, and things only got worse for Uncle Sam when Castro declared Cuba a socialist state, and then overnight became the Soviet Union's new best friend.

Batista had been a corrupt and repressive dictator, but he was pro-American, and most importantly of all he was reliably anti-communist. The last thing the U.S wanted was a new socialist state which was on first name terms with the Russian leadership, sitting less than 100 miles from its coast. The whole situation had American politicians as nervous as turkeys at Christmas time.

So the United States did what any Super-power would do when it wakes up one morning to find itself faced with a cigar smoking communist dictator running an Island country less than a stone's throw away. Officially the United States responded by severing diplomatic relations and prohibiting the importing of all things Cuban, but behind closed White House doors the Central Intelligence Agency (CIA) were quietly asked to find the quickest and most convenient way to have Castro assassinated.

Ever since, the CIA, along with numerous disgruntled Cuban-exile types, have tried to devise ways to assassinate Fidel Castro, but given that he's still happily blowing out the candles on his birthday cakes way into his 90's, all such attempts to-date have clearly fallen a little short of their primary mission objective.

Castro's seeming air of indestructibility is partly due to the fact that he appears to be luckier than a leprechaun, but mostly due to what appears to be the shear incompetence of the CIA and their attempts to end what is now for them Castro's embarrassingly lengthy residency as Chairman of the Board at Cuba HQ.

Many of the CIA's outlandish plots to bump off the Cuban dictator would not have appeared out of place in a James Bond spoof movie, having reportedly tried everything short of just nuking the entire country in shear desperation. Poison pens and pills, exploding cigars and shells, and outright bombing attempts have all been considered, yet failed. Once, presumably in an effort to appear helpful, Castro even offered a would-be assassin to shoot himself for them, but even this failed.

To date, conservative estimates for attempts on " El Commandante's" life are northwards of six hundred, which seems like a staggeringly high number, particularly when you consider that everyone single one has failed. But then Castro has always been a particularly prickly thorn in the side of Uncle Sam and thus a prime target, and whose presumably highly trained assassins, after over 600 attempts, have by now probably run out of new ways to even try and assassinate him.

While the exploding cigar trick that was intended to blow up in Castro's face is perhaps the best-known of the attempts on his life, others have been equally bizarre, and equally doomed to failure. Knowing his love for scuba-diving the CIA "ingeniously" planned to find a mollusc shell big enough to contain a lethal quantity of explosives, paint it in colours bright enough to attract Castro's attention while diving, and then detonate it. They even considered infecting his wet-suit with a fungus that would cause a chronic and debilitating skin disease, and eventually death. Neither plan it seems made it off the drawing board.

They've tried the usual text-book assassination approaches, with failed attempts using an under-cover agent with a pen-syringe, poison placed in Castro's handkerchief and coffee, approaching Mafia underworld figures to make him an offer he couldn't refuse, and even one time putting 200lbs of explosives under the podium where he was due to speak. But in each case the attempt was either foiled, or Castro somehow survived.

Even the infamous "Mata Hari" approach of using one of Castro's lovers was tried but with the same result. The lover was given poison pills by the CIA, which she hid in her cold-cream jar. Unfortunately, the pills melted in the cream and she decided that, all things considered, putting cold cream in Castro's mouth while he slept was never going to work. According to the former lover, Castro had anyway already guessed that she was aiming to kill him and had duly offered her his own pistol to do the job. However it seems she broke down at the last second, declaring "I can't do it, Fidel", and Castro lived, and presumably loved, another day.

It should come as no surprise then that by late 1960, fed up with waiting for reports of a successful assassination attempt to cross his desk, the then President of the United States, John F. Kennedy, decided it was time for a somewhat less subtle approach to removing Castro and his Socialist regime. Kennedy decided to go all-out old-school and put in motion plans for a full-scale invasion of Cuba.

Consequently, Kennedy agreed to a covert operation to overthrow Castro and his regime, to be planned and executed by the CIA. However, given the CIA's recent track record in trying to assassinate Castro, Kennedy should really have guessed that things were very likely not going to go well, and maybe with this in mind he insisted that whatever the plan, it must appear as if there was no direct participation or sponsorship by the United States.

The CIA advised Kennedy they could keep U.S. involvement in the invasion a secret as long as everyone only talked about it in whispers, and by using an army made up of only Cuban exiles as the invasion force. If all went according to plan, they assured, the campaign would quickly spark an anti-Castro uprising on the island, and Kennedy would be smoking Cuban cigars again within a matter of weeks.

However, true to recent CIA form, when the invasion occurred, nearly everything that could go wrong, did go wrong. It turned out to be a total fiasco. It quickly became apparent that the CIA's plan had been put together by a six year old, and rather than topple Castro the failed invasion attempt was to ultimately push the world to the brink of a nuclear Armageddon.

Things started to go wrong as soon as the mission started. The first part of the plan was to destroy Castro's Air-force, thus removing any threat to the invasion from the air, and so conveniently eliminating any embarrassing call for some U.S. air support by a panicked invasion force being blown out of the water even before it had landed.

Thus, on April 15, 1961, a group of Cuban exiles took off from Nicaragua in eight American B-26 bombers, which had been hastily dressed-up to look like stolen Cuban planes, and headed to Cuba to destroy the Cuban Air-force. However, having arrived over the Cuban air-fields with bombs at the ready, it turned out that Castro already knew about the raid and had moved most of his planes out of harm's way. The poorly disguised planes had a cargo-hold full of bombs but it seems with nothing even faintly resembling a Cuban Air-force to drop them on.

To make matters worse, Kennedy had initially agreed to supply sixteen planes for the mission, which was what military advisers considered to be the absolute bare minimum number necessary to destroy the Cuban Air-force. However, paranoid that American involvement would become too obvious, at the last minute Kennedy panicked and reduced the number to only eight.

Thus, not only was half the Cuban Air-force nowhere to be seen when the bombers arrived, they didn't have enough planes to do any real damage anyway. The plan had already failed at the first step, but it was already too late to apply the brakes.

On the night of April 17, the Cuban exile brigade began its invasion at an isolated spot on the island's southern shore known as the Bay of Pigs. The CIA had naturally wanted to keep the invasion a secret for as long as possible, but their lack of any reconnaissance of the area meant that they had failed to spot a radio station near the landing-beach, which almost immediately began to broadcast every detail of the landing operation to listeners across Cuba. The invasion had now become a soap-opera being played out across Cuba on the local radio.

By morning Cuba had mobilized and pinned down the American-trained forces on the beach, while the remaining Cuban Air-force attacked the four thinly disguised American supply ships just off the coast that were there to support the landing, causing two to sink and the other two to panic and flee back to Miami. The invasion force was now left stranded on the beach without supplies or support.

The military situation quickly deteriorated further for the stranded Cuban exiles over the next 48 hours. By April 18, while the fighting was at its peak, Kennedy was eventually persuaded to authorize unmarked U.S. fighter jets from the aircraft carrier Essex to provide escort cover for the invasion's B-26 bombers, most of which were now being flown by CIA agents in support of the ground invasion since the Cuban exile pilots were by now refusing to have anything to do with the invasion at all.

However, in one final humiliating act, the jets from the Essex missed their rendezvous with the B-26s by an hour as they had neglected to take into account the one hour time-zone difference between their U.S base and their planned rendezvous point. In the subsequent, unescorted bombing raid over Cuba, two of the B-26 bombers were shot down and four Americans were killed.

Severely lacking ammo and unable to escape from the beach, the landing-force were eventually forced to surrender red-faced after only three days. In the end, over 1,500 of the invasion force were captured and 114 were killed. Those captured were held in captivity for twenty months until the United States finally agreed to pay a sizable ransom to Cuba for their release. The whole invasion from start to embarrassing finish had utterly failed.

Most analysts later concluded that the planned invasion had been doomed to failure even before it started. Fidel Castro enjoyed wide support in Cuba and had just consolidated a military victory against the Batista regime with his highly trained and well equipped army. It is difficult to see how even the CIA could have envisioned a handful of disgruntled anti-Castro Cubans armed with a few rifles and some big sticks possibly taking the island by force.

Furthermore, the idea that the U.S. could keep either the invasion or its role in it a secret, had become ridiculous long before the invasion was even attempted. The New York Times had already run a story in March that year predicting a U.S. invasion of Cuba, and then in April it ran another story entitled "Anti-Castro Units Trained to Fight at Florida Bases," which noted that invasion plans were in their final stages. All a bit of a give-away. Effectively, Castro didn't need spies, all he had to do was read the newspapers.

For the U.S the incident proved rather embarrassing both at home and abroad. In the mess that ensued, the CIA and the Kennedy administration all wildly pointed accusing fingers at the other. Publicly, Kennedy accepted blame for the failure, but he personally blamed the CIA and his advisers, feeling a little like he'd ordered a sleek, covert, military operation, and instead got a disorganized band of disgruntled Cubans with pitch-forks, executing a plan that looked like it had been hastily planned over a few beers. For its part, the CIA was now publically seen as irresponsible, out-of-control, and incapable of planning a stag-party in a brothel, let alone a covert military invasion.

Supported by public outrage in Cuba over the U.S invasion, Castro himself merely consolidated his position, and in a clear case of self-preservation concluded a mutual-defence agreement with the Soviet Union, under which the Soviet Union happily placed nuclear missile sites on Cuban soil, each now pointing in the direction of Uncle Sam, just in case any clever six year olds at the CIA got anymore bright ideas.

Now, not only did the U.S have a communist state 90 miles from its shores, it now had one that also had Soviet nuclear missiles pointing in its direction. What was initially just an uncomfortable economic and political situation, had now escalated into a full-blown nuclear threat. At this point, it's difficult to think how things could have gone more wrong for the U.S.

The whole situation now quickly deteriorated into what became the Cuban Missile Crisis of 1962, which is generally agreed to have been the closest the world has so far come to an all-out nuclear war. For 13 days in October 1962, the leaders of the U.S. and the Soviet Union engaged in what was effectively a game of chicken with nuclear missiles.

The disaster was only avoided when someone helpfully pointed out that any full-scale use of high-yield nuclear missiles against each other would only result in the complete annihilation of both sides. Having realized they were both merely playing with the own "mutually assured destruction", both sides finally saw some sense.

The two Super-powers grudgingly shook hands and made up, with the Soviet Union agreeing to remove the Soviet missiles from Cuba in exchange for the U.S. promising not to try and invade Cuba again, with or without their own forces. The so called "Cold war" was effectively over, and the rest of the world stopped working on their bucket-lists and let out a collective sigh of relief.

Meanwhile, back in Cuba, Castro merely put his feet up on his desk, lit a fat Cuban cigar, sat back, smiled, and prepared to continue to be a thorn in America's side for the next 50 years.